SO-CAP-435

THE FACTS ON
JEHOVAH'S
WITNESSES

JOHN ANKERBERG
JOHN WELDON &
DILLON BURROUGHS

HARVEST HOUSE PUBLISHERS

EUGENE, OREGON

Cover by Dugan Design Group, Bloomington, Minnesota

Cover photos © iStockphoto

Back cover author(Dillon) photo © Goldberg Photography

THE FACTS ON JEHOVAH'S WITNESSES
Updated edition
Copyright © 1998/2008 by The John Ankerberg Theological Research Institute
Published by Harvest House Publishers
Eugene, Oregon 97402
www.harvesthousepublishers.com

Library of Congress Cataloging-in-Publication Data
Ankerberg, John, 1945-
     The facts on Jehovah's witnesses / John Ankerberg, John Weldon; updates by Dillon Burroughs.
          p. cm.—(Facts on series)
     Includes bibliographical references.
     ISBN 978-0-7369-2215-9
     1. Jehovah's Witnesses—Controversial literature. 2. Apologetics. I. Weldon, John. II. Burroughs, Dillon. III. Title.
     BX8526.5.A55 2008
     289.9'2—dc22

                                                                        2008001038

Printed in the United States of America

22 23 24 25 / VP-SK / 13 12 11 10 9

Contents

Section One
Introduction

Section Two
The Worldview of the Jehovah's Witnesses—
Practices and Teachings

Section Three
The Theology of the Jehovah's Witnesses

Section Four

Analysis and Critique—"Does God Speak Only Through the Watchtower Society?" Four Tests Examining This Claim

Test one: *If God speaks only through the Watchtower Society, then their Bible—the* New World Translation—*must be accurate. But is it?*

Test two: *If the Watchtower Society is the sole channel for God on earth, then according to the Bible, its prophecies must come true. How reliable have its prophecies been?*

Test three: *If the Watchtower Society is God's sole channel for communication on earth, then its scholarship should be trustworthy—but is it?*

Test four: *If the Watchtower Society admits it received many of its teachings from angels or spirits and those teachings have proven to be false, is such a source trustworthy?*

Section Five
Conclusion

Introduction

1

Who are the Jehovah's Witnesses?

The Jehovah's Witnesses are a religious movement started by Charles Taze Russell in the late 1870s. In formulating their beliefs, Russell drew from many sources, including the religious teachings of the Seventh-Day Adventist church, Christadelphianism, and his own interpretation of the Bible.[1] Through aggressive door-to-door proselytizing and authoritarian leadership, the group has grown from a small number of students to allegedly more than 7 million members in over 200 countries and territories.[2]

2

Who are the leaders of the Jehovah's Witnesses?

The leaders of the Jehovah's Witnesses are a group of men who head an organization called the Watchtower Bible and Tract Society, or simply the Watchtower Society, in Brooklyn, New York. This small group wields absolute spiritual authority over the members. To date, the Society has had six presidents, each of whom has left his unique mark on the Society's religion.

3

How have the Watchtower Society's presidents shaped the organization?

Each president of the Jehovah's Witnesses has

governed authoritatively. As a result, his period of rule has been marked by his unique personality and Bible interpretation. Thus there have been six distinct "periods" of the Society: 1) the period of Charles Taze Russell (1872–1916); 2) the period of "Judge" Joseph F. Rutherford (1917–1942); 3) the period of Nathan H. Knorr (1942–1977); 4) the period of Frederick W. Franz (1977–1992); 5) the period of Milton G. Henschel (1992–2000); and 6) the period of Don Adams (2000–present).

Because the Witnesses claim that God himself was and is the source or author of all their Bible interpretations and doctrines, it is important to briefly discuss these six periods. Doing so reveals the fact that each president has interpreted the Bible *differently* or even in *contradiction* to one or more of the others. Examining the writings of these men clearly shows that the claim of the Jehovah's Witnesses that God is the author of all of the Watchtower Society's doctrines is inaccurate.

Not of God

The Bible teaches that "God is not a God of confusion but of peace" (1 Corinthians 14:33 NASB). This is the first item of evidence that reveals that the Watchtower Society is guided not by God, but by fallible men.

Charles Taze Russell

Examples of this start with Charles Taze Russell, the Society's founder, who wrote a new Bible for the faithful of his day. In it, he claimed the translation "came from God through the enlightenment of the Holy Spirit."[3] This was the seven-volume *Studies in the Scriptures*.[4] He insisted this material was absolutely necessary for a proper understanding of the Bible. In the Society's primary publication, the *Watchtower* magazine, Russell stated categorically that without *Studies in the Scriptures* a person could never "see the divine plan in studying the Bible by itself." Further, he made the incredible claim that even after reading *Studies in the Scriptures* for ten years, if a person stopped reading it and went to "the Bible alone," that "within two years he [would revert] into darkness." On the other hand, a person who never read the Bible but only read Russell's volumes "would be in the light at the end of two years because he would have had the light of the Scriptures."[5] In other words, Russell claimed that a new divine interpreter was needed to understand the Bible properly. And he claimed to be that interpreter.

Yet today's leaders of the Watchtower Society contradict many of Russell's doctrines and "divine interpretations" of Scripture. Apparently, the true "divine interpreter" has changed. It is now no longer Russell but the Watchtower Society itself. It still claims the same authority Russell did: that only its interpretations of the Bible are authoritative, and if a person studies the Bible alone it will lead to darkness and heresy. For example, a 1981 issue of the *Watchtower* condemns those who

> say that it is sufficient to read the Bible exclusively, either alone or in small groups at home. Through such "Bible reading," they have reverted right back to the apostate doctrines that commentaries by Christendom's clergy were teaching 100 years ago.[6]

Notice that the Watchtower Society itself declares, as did Russell, that anyone who reads the Bible alone will come to the same beliefs orthodox Christians have always held. Nevertheless, the writings Russell once called indispensable for understanding the Bible (his own) are today largely ignored by the organization he founded.

The problem with reading just the Bible

Cal Lehman, a former 35-year Jehovah's Witness, noted, "The more Bible reading I did, without Watchtower publications to stir my thinking, the more errors I began to see in the teachings of the Watchtower." His comment is only one of many such examples.[7]

J.F. Rutherford

Under the direction of the second president, "Judge" Rutherford, the Watchtower Society became even more authoritarian. Rutherford instituted an era of changes and ignored, altered, or denied hundreds or thousands of Russell's teachings. He justified these changes by claiming an ongoing revelation that permitted him to shed new light on Russell's ideas.[8]

This is why thousands of faithful followers of Russell, realizing Rutherford had abandoned Russell's teaching, left the organization. They still believed Russell's claim that he was inspired by God and felt that to change his teachings was to deny God. The broad majority of Witnesses, however, accepted the vast changes without many questions.

Nathan H. Knorr

During the third major era, under the organizational leadership of Nathan H. Knorr, the number of Witnesses grew from 105,000 to about 2.2 million. New stress was placed on training in the Jehovah's Witnesses' own interpretations of the Bible. A new Bible translation was produced to support their interpretations—and with it came additional changes in Bible interpretation and doctrine.[9]

Frederick W. Franz

The fourth era, under Frederick W. Franz, could be labeled an era of crisis because thousands of Witnesses began to examine the history of the Watchtower Society independently. As a result, they became convinced that it was not God's organization and either left it or were disfellowshipped.

President Franz's nephew, Raymond, is an example of one who has left the Watchtower. His book *Crisis of Conscience* shows why the Watchtower Society cannot be God's sole channel on earth. His text is an authoritative exposé by a key leader familiar with the inner workings of the Watchtower Society. It portrays an authoritarian group of men who go to great lengths to retain their image of divine guidance. Raymond Franz concludes that the Watchtower Society is not of God. He cites evidence that it 1) is antibiblical, 2) has given extensive false prophecies, 3) has changed its teachings and policies, 4) has engaged in lying and cover-ups, and 5) has brought destruction into the lives of some of its members.[10] "Most of the [Governing] Body were actually not that well versed in the Scriptures," he writes. They practiced "manipulation of Scripture and fact" to uphold their interpretations of the Bible. The emphasis was "not loyalty to God and His Word, but loyalty to the organization and its teachings."[11]

The Society has reacted to those who question its authority with the spiritual threat of disfellowshipping. For most Jehovah's Witnesses, disfellowshipping means friends and family in the Watchtower cannot associate with you, and it deprives you of any chance of salvation in this life (see also page 35).

Milton G. Henschel and Don Adams

The fifth president, Milton G. Henschel, stepped down in 2000 after only eight years, in the midst of a restructuring of the organization. Henschel's successor, Don Adams, became the Watchtower Society's sixth president in October 2000. The overall impact of his leadership remains to be seen.

4

What attracts people to the Jehovah's Witnesses?

Many people are attracted to the Jehovah's Witnesses because they claim to have authoritative answers to many of life's problems. In a society torn by relative values and personal insecurities, any group is attractive that 1) claims to offer divine guidance, 2) claims to provide genuine solutions to life's problems, and 3) stresses moral and family values. The Watchtower Society is appealing to people who are looking for answers, who are frightened about the future, or who are tired of the lack of moral values in America. They are drawn to the dedication and commitment that the Witnesses show.

In addition, many people in liberal mainline churches who feel they have an inadequate level of Bible knowledge have a desire to know it better. They are grateful for the Witnesses, who devote a lot of time and effort to allegedly helping them understand what the Bible teaches on life's issues.

The Worldview of the
Jehovah's Witnesses—
Practices and Teachings

5

What is the religious worldview of the Jehovah's Witnesses, and what logical results flow from it?

Three basic beliefs or assumptions form the religious worldview of the Jehovah's Witnesses:

a) Divine guidance comes only through the Watchtower Society. This assumption leads Witnesses to live under an authoritarian organization that suppresses independent thinking in the name of God. Once a member accepts the organization's policies and decisions as being God's will, disagreement with the Watchtower Society is disagreement with God. The consequence is that any criticism of the Watchtower Society is defined as sinful or even satanic. The Society teaches that "Jehovah's organization is in no wise [way] democratic. His government or organization is strictly theocratic" (which means ruled by God alone).[1]

b) Jehovah's Witnesses alone have the truth of God. They alone are the people of God. This follows logically from their first assumption that divine guidance comes only from the Watchtower. This belief causes an attitude of exclusivism that stresses their uniqueness and superiority. This in turn leads them to accept an alleged divine command to be separate from the entire world system—social, political, military, and religious. Witnesses view the whole world system and other churches as satanic.

The Watchtower tells them with alleged divine

authority that Jehovah's Witnesses are to be separatists and are to renounce activities such as military service, patriotism, and celebrating religious holidays (see question 7). Children of Jehovah's Witnesses are not permitted to engage in school activities prohibited by the Watchtower Society—such as Christmas plays, saluting the flag, and reciting the Pledge of Allegiance—which sometimes leads to their being ostracized by their peers.

c) *Jehovah's Witnesses are told that Orthodox, Protestant, and Catholic Christianity are false and controlled by Satan.* Because of this belief, Witnesses often avoid Christians and completely reject their concept of the Christian faith (see question 8).

6

Does the Watchtower Society really claim to be the only organization on earth through which God works?

The Watchtower Society does claim that of all religious organizations, God works only through it. It alone has authority to speak for God.[2] For example, the *Watchtower* states,

> We belong to NO earthly organization. We adhere only to that heavenly organization. All the saints now living or that ever lived during this age, belong to OUR CHURCH ORGANIZATION: such are all ONE CHURCH, and there is NO OTHER recognized by the Lord.[3]

Thus, Jehovah's Witnesses believe that no one on earth can discover the complete will of God apart from the Watchtower Society. It is only the Watchtower Society and its publications that can reveal the true meaning of the Bible. The Society is seen as "God's sole collective channel for the flow of biblical truth to men on earth."[4]

Unfinished revelation

One Jehovah's Witness said to a Christian, "Your Bible was finished 2000 years ago, but our Bible has 32 pages added to it every week." He was referring to the *Watchtower* magazine, which Witnesses are taught is for all practical purposes the Word of God.[5]

A former member wrote,

> We were taught that we must adhere absolutely to the decisions and scriptural understandings of the Society, because God had given it this authority over His people (the *Watchtower,* May 10, 1972, p. 272). To gain…eternal life, I was told certain things were necessary: (1) I should study the Bible diligently, and only through Watchtower publications…[6]

A 1983 *Watchtower* stated as a requirement of salvation "that we be associated with God's channel, His organization. To receive everlasting life in the earthly paradise we must identify that organization and serve God as part of it."[7]

From the above statements, it is clear that the Watchtower Society claims to be the only organization on earth through which God works and through which a person can receive everlasting life in their concept of an earthly paradise.

7

Why do Jehovah's Witnesses prohibit practices like military service, saluting the flag, celebrating holidays, and blood transfusions?

These and many other practices are prohibited because the entire world system, apart from activity in the Watchtower organization, is believed to be connected with the devil. Military service, patriotism, and celebrating holidays are allegedly all part of the devil's scheme to lead men away from God. For example the Watchtower Society asks, "Do you want to be part of Satan's world or are you for God's new system?...Getting out of Babylon the Great, the world empire of false religion...also means having nothing to do with the religious celebrations of the world."[8]

Other practices are prohibited because they are wrongly thought to be prohibited by Scripture. Although the Bible only forbids *eating* blood (something associated with pagan rituals), the Watchtower Society has wrongly interpreted this as a ban on blood *transfusions*, something entirely different. Jehovah's Witnesses teach that accepting a blood transfusion may "cost...[one his] eternal life...."[9] Tragically, many Jehovah's Witnesses and their children have died because they have believed the Watchtower's view on blood transfusions.[10] However, there have been various reports that suggest a change in doctrine may be under way, despite the fact that the official Watchtower Society website still retains the statement that members "refuse to accept blood" transfusions.[11] The Watchtower Society may have, incrementally, begun to lift its ban, with the current teaching that certain unique blood products may be used in some cases. However, the traditional Jehovah's Witness teaching of refusing blood transfusions continues to stand for now, even though thousands of Jehovah's Witnesses and their children continue to die.

8

What do Jehovah's Witnesses believe about Christianity?

Not surprisingly, the Jehovah's Witnesses believe Christianity is an apostate religion that has taught false doctrines and deceived people for over 1,800 years. Until Jehovah's Witnesses appeared in the late nineteenth century and began teaching the Bible correctly, God's truth was largely absent from the world. As a result, Jehovah's Witnesses believe that the Christian church is a satanic deception and that they alone are the true church.

Consider the following statements that have been made by some of the Watchtower presidents and official leaders:[13]

- "Jehovah's Christian Witnesses are the ones that have identified who Babylon the Great is...the world empire of false religion. The chief component member and mouthpiece in that religious world empire is Christendom! She is the most reprehensible member thereof because she claims to be 'Christian.' Her blasphemies exceed those of 'pagandom.'...Her blood guilt exceeds that of all the non-Christian religious realm."

- "Christendom's course is 'the way of death.' "

- "The Anglo-American empire system, which

chiefly is 'Christendom,' Satan makes his chief spokesman on earth."

- "Christendom's religion is demonism."

- "As the most reprehensible ones among the people of Christendom, the clergy and religious leaders will drink the potion of death."

It is clear from these quotes that Jehovah's Witnesses view Christians and the Christian faith as one of their most powerful enemies. Does this mean they have compassion on Christians and hope to rescue them from their collision course with God's judgment? Do they take Jesus seriously and love their enemies (Matthew 5:44)? While some do, Watchtower Society literature has offered sentiments that sometimes indicate the opposite:

> Haters of God and His people…are to be hated. We must hate in the truest sense, which is to regard with extreme and active aversion, to consider as loathsome, odious, filthy, to detest. Surely any haters of God are not fit to live on this beautiful earth…We must have a proper perspective of these enemies…we cannot love those hateful enemies, for they are fit only for destruction…We pray with intensity and plead that [Jehovah's] anger be made manifest…Oh, Jehovah God of Hosts be not merciful to any wicked transgressors…consume them in wrath, consume them that they shall be no more.[14]

Regardless of these views, when Jehovah's Witnesses go door-to-door, this presents the perfect opportunity for Christians to show them Christ's love. To do this effectively, however, it is important to understand what the Witnesses believe and why it is not biblical. It is also important to help them begin to question the authority claims of the Watchtower Society.

The Theology of the Jehovah's Witnesses

9

What do Jehovah's Witnesses believe about God and the doctrine of the Trinity?

Jehovah's Witnesses believe that the God of Christianity is a false and satanic counterfeit of the one true God, Jehovah. Former President Charles Taze Russell even wrote that the Christian God was "the devil himself."[1] Jehovah's Witnesses see God as a single person, not as a single Being in whom are united three Persons, as Christians view God. They also deny that God is present everywhere and limit His omniscience.[2]

Because the Watchtower Society teaches that God is only one person, Witnesses reject the biblical teaching of the Trinity as an invention of "pagan imagination." They call it "a false doctrine…promulgated [put forth] by Satan for the purposes of defaming Jehovah's name."[3]

Five statements about the Trinity

The Watchtower Society may sometimes accurately depict the doctrine of the Trinity or may sometimes misrepresent the teaching in its publications. Biblical Christianity does not teach that there are "three Gods" or "a complicated, freakish-looking, three-headed God."[4] Instead, the Bible teaches that the one true God exists eternally as three Persons. The doctrine of the Trinity can be seen from five simple statements supported by the Bible, even the mistranslated Bible of the Watchtower:[5]

1. *There is only one true God.* "For there is one God, and one mediator between God and men" (1 Timothy 2:5 *NWT*; compare Deuteronomy 4:35; 6:4; Isaiah 43:10).

2. *The Father is God.* "There is actually to us one God the Father" (1 Corinthians 8:6 *NWT*; compare John 17:1-3; 2 Corinthians 1:3; Philippians 2:11; Colossians 1:3; 1 Peter 1:2).

3. *Jesus Christ, the Son, is God.* "But he [Jesus] was also calling God his own Father, making himself equal to God" (John 5:18 *NWT*); "In answer Thomas said to him [Jesus]: 'My Lord and my God!'" (John 20:28 *NWT*; compare Isaiah 9:6; John 1:1; Romans 9:5; Titus 2:13; 2 Peter 1:1).

Decades of unacknowledged changes

Beyond its distortion of the meaning of the original Greek, the *New World Translation* has undergone hundreds of revisions since the 1930s, when it was developed. Nearly all of these changes are not acknowledged by the Watchtower Society, which makes them in order to fit the *NWT* to doctrinal changes or, in some cases, to avoid further embarrassment over errors.

In this book, unless otherwise noted we are quoting and referring to an edition of the *NWT* found on the Watchtower Society's Web site (www.watchtower.org). It is marked with the copyright date of 2006, and we accessed it in March of 2008.

4. *The Holy Spirit is a Person, is eternal, and is therefore God.* The Holy Spirit is a *Person:* "However, when that one arrives, the spirit of the truth, *he* will guide YOU into all the truth, for *he* will not speak of *his* own impulse, but what things *he* hears *he* will speak, and *he* will declare to YOU the things coming" (John 16:13 *NWT*, emphasis added). The Holy Spirit is *eternal:* "How much more will the blood of the Christ, who through an everlasting spirit offered himself without blemish

to God" (Hebrews 9:14 *NWT*). The Holy Spirit is therefore *God:* "But Peter said: 'Ananias, why has Satan emboldened you to play false to the holy spirit?...You have played false, not to men, but to God'" (Acts 5:3-4 *NWT*).

5. *The Father, Son, and Holy Spirit are distinct Persons....* "baptizing them in the name of the Father and of the Son and of the holy spirit"; "The undeserved kindness of the Lord Jesus Christ and the love of God and the sharing in the holy spirit be with all of YOU" (Matthew 28:19; 2 Corinthians 13:14 *NWT*).

It is clear from these verses, whether read from the *New World Translation* or a modern version like the New International Version, that the Bible teaches that one true God exists eternally as Father, Son, and Holy Spirit. For 1,900 years the historic Christian church has found in the Bible the doctrine of the Trinity as defined above. This can also be seen by anyone who reads the Church Fathers and studies the historic creeds.[6]

An "unreasonable" doctrine?

Humanity's incomplete comprehension of this truth is no reason to reject what Scripture teaches, as the Watchtower Society itself agrees:

> Sincere seekers for the truth want to know what is right. They realize they would only be fooling themselves if they rejected portions of God's Word while claiming to base their beliefs on other parts.[7]

Nevertheless, Jehovah's Witnesses allow fallible human reason to judge God's infallible Word. They reject the Bible's teaching about the one true God existing as three

Persons and replace it with their own view that God is only one Person. Because the idea of a triune God is "unreasonable" to them, they think it cannot be true.[8]

To see how unreasonable the Witnesses are in thinking this way, let's consider an illustration from science. Scientists long believed that light existed as either *waves* or *particles*—two contradictory things. They felt it could not possibly be both because their natures were different. But modern scientific tests surprised scientists and indicated to them that light exists as both waves *and* particles. For a while some couldn't accept this conclusion because it didn't seem reasonable. Some scientists insisted that light was only waves, while others insisted that it was only particles. Finally, though, scientists were forced by the evidence to conclude that light really was both waves *and* particles. Rather than clinging illogically to their preconceived notions of reality, they were forced by the evidence to accept a different conclusion.

No scientist completely understands this fact or can explain it in full detail. But all of them are honest enough to accept that this is the nature of light. In the same way, God has told us who he is. The evidence of Scripture leads us to accept that the one true God exists as Father, Son, and Holy Spirit. We may not be able to fully understand it or explain every detail, but we accept it because this is what the facts have brought us to believe.

Another illustration is love. No one really *understands* what love is, how it works, how it begins, how it grows, or anything else connected with it. Yet we don't question its reality merely because we can't fully understand it.

Jehovah's Witnesses don't deny the reality of light or love merely because they don't fully understand them.

Why, then, do they insist they must understand God before they accept his existence as he has revealed it?

The Trinity is integral within Scripture

Father, Son, and Holy Spirit are so effortlessly and consistently linked in Scripture that assuming God is not three Persons makes it impossible to understand some passages (for example, Matthew 28:19; 2 Corinthians 1:21-22; 13:14; Ephesians 2:18; 3:11-16; 5:18-20; 1 Thessalonians 1:1-5).

Further, how could we answer the following questions without concluding that the Bible teaches the Trinity?

1. *Who raised Jesus from the dead?* The Father (Romans 6:4; Acts 3:26; 1 Thessalonians 1:10)? The Son (John 2:19-21; 10:17-18)? The Holy Spirit (Romans 8:11)? Or God (Hebrews 13:20; Acts 13:30; 17:31)?

2. *Who does the Bible say is God?* The Father (Ephesians 4:6)? The Son (Titus 2:13; John 1:1; 20:28)? The Holy Spirit (Acts 5:3-4)? The one and only true God (Deuteronomy 4:35)?

3. *Who created the universe?* The Father (John 14:2)? The Son (Colossians 1:16-17; John 1:1-3)? The Holy Spirit (Genesis 1:2; Psalm 104:30)? Or God (Genesis 1:1; Hebrews 11:3)?

4. *Who saves people? Who redeems people?* The Father (1 Peter 1:3)? The Son (John 5:21; 4:14)? The Holy Spirit (John 3:6; Titus 3:5)? Or God (1 John 3:9)? *Who justifies people and makes them right with God?* The Father (Jeremiah 23:6, compare 2 Corinthians 5:19)? The Son (Romans 5:9; 10:4;

2 Corinthians 5:19,21)? The Holy Spirit (1 Corinthians 6:11; Galatians 5:5)? Or God (Romans 4:6; 9:33)? *Who sets apart people?* The Father (Jude 1)? The Son (Titus 2:14)? The Holy Spirit (1 Peter 1:2)? Or God (Exodus 31:13)? *Who propitiated God's just anger against people for their sins?* The Father (1 John 4:14; John 3:16; 17:5; 18:11)? The Son (Matthew 26:28; John 1:29; 1 John 2:2)? The Holy Spirit (Hebrews 9:14)? Or God (2 Corinthians 5:1; Acts 20:28)?

Though Jehovah's Witnesses exalt human reason against the doctrine of the Trinity, claiming it is "unreasonable," people who base their beliefs on the teachings found in God's Word must conclude that it is unreasonable *not* to believe in the Trinity. As Dr. Walter Martin, author of the standard text *Kingdom of the Cults,* once stated in an interview I (John Ankerberg) conducted,

> For you to say you won't believe what God says in his Word because you don't understand it means you are saying you are smarter than God, who told you. For you to comprehend all God says, you would have to be God—and you're not.[9]

10

What do Jehovah's Witnesses believe about Jesus?

The Jehovah's Witnesses teach that Jesus Christ was the first creation of God, the archangel Michael. They believe that he "had a beginning" and "was actually a creature of God."[10] By so believing, Jehovah's Witnesses reject the Bible's teaching about Jesus.

The Bible teaches that although Christ is fully man, he is also fully God (John 1:1; 5:18; 10:30; 20:28; Titus 2:13; Colossians 2:9; Philippians 2:1-8). It teaches that, as God, Christ is eternal, not created (Micah 5:2; John 1:1-3). All these verses the *New World Translation* mistranslates to sustain its views (for examples, see question 14).

Jehovah's Witnesses incorrectly teach that "Christ Jesus received immortality as a reward for his faithful course of action" on earth. This is because "any failure on his part would have meant eternal death [extinction] for him."[11]

However, the Bible teaches something completely different. It teaches that, as God, Jesus was already immortal and could never have ceased to exist; he is the same yesterday, today, and forever (Hebrews 13:8). He did not have to earn his own salvation because he was always sinless (Hebrews 4:15) and immortal (Isaiah 9:6) and did not need salvation.

Re-creation, not resurrection

Jehovah's Witnesses deny the physical resurrection of Christ (John 2:19-21; 1 Corinthians 15:3-4,17,35-49), teaching instead that when God allegedly re-created Jesus, he made him an immortal angel. Jesus no longer existed, and the new "Michael" had no access to Jesus' earthly body. As Russell wrote, "The man Jesus is dead, forever dead."[12]

Altered identity?

According to the teachings of the Jehovah's Witnesses, though, the fundamental identity of Jesus has been altered. They believe the archangel Michael was changed into the mortal man Jesus, and at that point ceased to exist as an angel. Later the man Jesus was changed into an improved and immortal version of the archangel Michael. This happened when God re-created the man Jesus after his death.

But this differs greatly from the writings of the apostle Paul. Writing about Jesus' death and resurrection, Paul taught that there "*is* one God and one mediator between God and men, the *man* Christ Jesus" (1 Timothy 2:5). Ultimately, Jehovah's Witnesses deny the biblical teaching that Jesus is "the same yesterday and today and forever" (Hebrews 13:8).[13] They also deny the title "Son of Man," used by Jesus 81 times in the Gospels about himself. He used this phrase to teach that he was fully man and fully God. Just a study of how Jesus used this title in referring to himself defeats the Jehovah's Witnesses' teaching.

A physical, visible reality

Finally, because Jehovah's Witnesses teach that after Jesus' death he ceased to exist and God re-created him immortal as a spirit creature (Michael, an angel), it is impossible that Jesus could ever return to earth visibly and physically as he taught he would. Rather, Jehovah's Witnesses teach that Michael returned *invisibly* in 1914.[14] But the Bible does not teach that Michael once stopped existing and was later re-created again or that he will take Jesus' place in returning to the earth. Rather, the Bible reveals that someday Jesus will return in a cataclysmic event and the entire world will recognize him (Matthew 24:1-35). The Bible says Jesus will appear visibly, not invisibly; and physically, not spiritually, to all of the world.

Further, when Jesus comes in the air to rapture, or catch up, Christians, the Bible says, "The Lord himself will come down from heaven, with a loud command, with the voice of the archangel and with the trumpet call of God, and the dead in Christ will rise first" (1 Thessalonians 4:16). Notice it is Jesus, the Lord, who returns. The name of the archangel who speaks in a loud voice is not mentioned. The Bible teaches that Jesus will appear in the same body he had while on the earth, although now glorified (John 20:24-28; Acts 1:9-11; Zechariah 12:10). In sum, the Christ of the Jehovah's Witnesses is not the Christ of the Bible.

11

What do Jehovah's Witnesses believe about salvation?

Salvation is claimed to be different for different people

Jehovah's Witnesses believe that there are three classes of people who will be saved by good works. But each class is working to gain a different salvation and exist in a different geographical place.

The first class of individuals is an extremely small group of people the Jehovah's Witnesses call the 144,000. Only these are elected by God for special spiritual privileges and to go to heaven when they die. For example, many of the blessings the Bible teaches are given to *every* believer by faith alone (that is, to billions of believers throughout history) are, according to the Watchtower Society, reserved exclusively for 144,000 Jehovah's Witnesses. The 144,000 are said to enjoy the spiritual privileges and blessings of justification and being born again. However, in Watchtower theology, *justification* and being *born again* are redefined.

Biblically justification is a once-for-all legal declaration God makes about a believer at the point of faith in Christ, giving him a perfect and righteous standing before God on account of the atonement of Christ, as is taught in Scripture (Romans 3:28; Philippians 3:9). To the contrary, Jehovah's Witnesses claim that justification is a "present justification" that may be forfeited at any time by disobedience.[15]

The Watchtower also redefines the words *born again*. Jehovah's Witnesses teach that being born again is being water baptized and anointed by God so the 144,000 may be re-created by God as spirit creatures after death, just as God supposedly re-created Jesus as the angel Michael after his death. (Thus, the Witnesses teach that Jesus was born again at his baptism.) The 144,000 are spiritually privileged to eventually be re-created like Jesus, and also privileged to rule with Jesus in heaven.[16]

Sadly, Jehovah's Witnesses do not understand that the Bible really teaches that *all* people, not just the 144,000, can be born again and go to heaven. They do not realize that being born again is a spiritual rebirth in the inner person that God grants, a rebirth that can occur during life and that brings with it eternal life, not on earth, but in heaven (John 3:3-8; 5:24; 6:47; in the *NWT*: John 1:11-13; 2 Corinthians 5:1; 1 John 1:1-3; 1 Peter 1:3-4).

The second class of individuals includes all other Jehovah's Witnesses (called "the other sheep"). According to Watchtower doctrine, they cannot be justified in this life, nor can they be born again. As a result, contrary to the Bible, the average Jehovah's Witness has no hope of and no interest in ever being born again or going to heaven. At death God does not re-create these people as spirit beings, as Jesus was changed into Michael, but re-creates their physical bodies to live only on the earth. These people are told they will be ruled over by Jesus (Michael) and the 144,000 who will live in heaven.

We had a mother and daughter on our television program who were former Jehovah's Witnesses. The mother had believed she was one of the 144,000 who would go to heaven. Her daughter had believed she was like all other Jehovah's Witnesses and would have to remain on earth. She was mad at God for separating them eternally. Later, they both became Christians and realized how cruel this Watchtower doctrine was.

The third class of individuals includes non–Jehovah's Witnesses who have lived good enough lives to be given the opportunity to earn salvation after death (a teaching the Bible denies—Hebrews 9:27). All who are worthy of this second chance will be re-created by Jehovah to live in the new millennium. But they will gain life beyond the millennium only if they attain perfection during it.[17] That's 1,000 years of obedient living! This is not salvation by grace, but by works.

None of the above three categories fits the teachings found in the Bible. God's Word says there is only one basis upon which God grants salvation, and it is offered freely to all people—men and women, mothers, fathers, and children (Galatians 1:6-8; John 3:16; Acts 4:12). Again, the new birth and heavenly salvation are not limited to 144,000 people, but are given freely to every believer: "Believe on the Lord Jesus Christ and you will get saved" (Acts 16:31 NWT). Salvation is by grace through faith alone, not by any of our works of righteousness (Ephesians 2:8-9; Titus 3:5; Romans 3:28 NWT). In fact, because salvation is "by grace [God's unmerited favor], then it is no longer by works [by goodness, merit, and works]; if it were, grace would no longer be grace" (Romans 11:6).

Jesus declared to *all* people, "You must be born again." He warned that no one could be acceptable to

God without a spiritual rebirth in this life that comes through faith in him (John 3:3-18). He warned, "Unless you believe that I am He, you will die in your sins" (John 8:24 NASB).*

Salvation is by personal merit and good works, not by grace through faith

For a Jehovah's Witness, grace is merely the opportunity for a person to earn his or her own salvation by works. It is not the free gift of God. Because Jehovah's Witnesses think they must earn their own salvation, they have no concept of true biblical grace.[18] Grace for them is simply the fact that God has given them a way to work their way to paradise. Jehovah's Witnesses teach that obeying "God's commandments can mean an eternal future,"[19] but this cannot give any *assurance* of salvation or that a person will enter heaven:

> In all areas of life, we should be prepared to give our very best. We should not be half-hearted about such vital matters. What is at stake is Jehovah's approval and our being granted life.[20]

As with all work systems of salvation, one always has to wonder if he or she did enough to be accepted. The Bible, in direct contrast, teaches that no person's good works can earn salvation (Romans 3:10-20 NWT). The Bible says that salvation cannot be earned or maintained by personal works of righteousness (Galatians 2:16,21 NWT). It is available only to those who recognize they are unworthy and cannot earn it, who in repentance turn from sin and place their faith in Christ's work at the cross for them (Romans 3:22; Luke 18:9-14 NWT).

---

* Here he applies "He" to himself—the divine name that God called himself in the Old Testament. Compare Exodus 3:14; Isaiah 43:10.

Over and over the Watchtower is falsely teaching its people that God justifies people only "on the basis of their own merit," that salvation rests wholly on their own good works, obedience to God, and personal merit. If they perform inadequately or mess up (also called backsliding), their salvation is forfeited and they risk being annihilated forever.[21]

This means that the only salvation a Jehovah's Witness has is the desperate hope that somehow as a fallen and sinful human being, their own personal efforts will at some point finally win God's approval. But only constant, diligent battling against sin—and total obedience to serving God through the Watchtower—offer a person any hope of being re-created after death for millennial life. Even then, Jehovah's Witnesses teach that during the millennium it is very possible to fail and then be annihilated. If a person serves faithfully all through this 1,000-year period of time, he or she may finally win eternal life. But it will be only because he has earned it by personal effort and merit.

The better news from the Bible

But the good news for every Jehovah's Witness is that God, in the Bible, directly opposes the Watchtower's plan of salvation. In the Bible, God himself *guarantees* eternal life. The eternal life he promises to give does not begin in a distant future but the very moment a person believes in Christ for forgiveness of sins. As even the *New World Translation* notes,

> Most truly I say to YOU, He that hears my word and believes him that sent me *has* [at that moment] everlasting life, and he does *not* come into judgment [in the future] but *has* passed over from death to life [now] (John 5:24 *NWT*, emphasis added).

Most truly I say to YOU, He that believes *has* everlasting life (John 6:47 *NWT*, emphasis added).

At the very moment a person accepts the work of Christ on his behalf and asks Jesus to save him, he is born again and made a new creation (John 3:1-16; 2 Corinthians 5:17).

For this is the will of my Father, that *everyone* [notice: this is not just the 144,000, but everyone] that beholds the Son and exercises faith in him should have everlasting life, and I *will* resurrect him at the last day (John 6:40 *NWT*, emphasis added).

Even the *New World Translation* declares that salvation is "not owing to YOU, it is God's gift" (Ephesians 2:8 *NWT*). By definition, a gift cannot be paid for. The *Oxford American Dictionary* defines a gift as "a thing given or received without payment."

It just doesn't follow...

No husband takes flowers home to his wife and says, "Hi, honey. These are yours when you wash the car." In the same way, no one pays for salvation with his or her works when it has been freely given as a gift.

God says he is giving eternal life as a free gift, a gift he can offer because he sent Jesus to purchase it. The *New World Translation* says, "But the *gift* God gives is everlasting life by Christ Jesus our Lord" (Romans 6:23 *NWT*, emphasis added). Further, the *NWT* emphatically declares, "By this *undeserved* kindness, indeed, YOU *have been saved through faith;* and this *not* owing to YOU, it is God's *gift*. No, *it is not owing to works,* in order that no man should have grounds for boasting" (Ephesians 2:8-9 *NWT*, emphasis added).

Analysis and Critique— "Does God Speak Only Through the Watchtower Society?"

Four Tests Examining This Claim

No question is more vital to an individual Jehovah's Witness than whether the Watchtower Society is really God's sole channel for communicating his will to people today. When we listen to the Watchtower Society, are we really listening to God? If we are, then we should listen carefully. But if we're not, then we should reject what it says when it claims to speak for God.

There are four key tests by which we may investigate whether or not the Watchtower Society is God's *only* channel for communicating His will to people today. If God does communicate to all people through the Watchtower Society, then each of the following four test inquiries should be answered in a manner consistent with its claims.

TEST ONE

If God speaks only through the Watchtower Society, then their Bible—the New World Translation—*must be accurate. But is it? (The next three questions examine the* NWT.*)*

12

Do Jehovah's Witnesses claim that the *New World Translation* is accurate?

The Watchtower claims that its translation of the Bible is highly accurate, and that the *New World Translation* is one of the most accurate translations yet produced. As it states, "The translation must be appraised on its own merits."[1] (From these words the Jehovah's Witnesses clearly invite outsiders to examine the *NWT*'s accuracy.) In the publication *All Scripture Is Inspired by God and Beneficial*, the Watchtower claims precise grammatical accuracy in translation and adds that "the *New World Translation*…is accurate and reliable…a faithful translation of God's word."[2]

Within the volume of the *New World Translation* itself, the Watchtower claims it has translated the Scriptures "as accurately as possible," with both a fear of and love for God—indeed with a great "sense of solemn responsibility."[3]

The spread of the NWT

According to watchtower.org, as of 2008, the *NWT* was available in all or part in 71 languages, making for a total of 143 million copies.

The Kingdom Interlinear Translation of the Greek Scriptures, which shows the Greek text and the *NWT* text side by side, claims that its New Testament translation accurately renders "what the original language says and means"—and that it does so in an unbiased way, "without any sectarian religious coloration."[4]

The Watchtower Society has even gone so far as to say that God himself has supervised its translation of the Bible by "angels of various ranks who controlled" the translators.

Society president F.W. Franz, along with then-president Nathan Knorr, headed the secret committee of seven translators. Franz testified in a court case in Edinburgh, Scotland, November 23, 1954. The *Scottish Daily Express* on November 24, 1954, recorded his testimony word for word concerning the *New World Translation.* In his testimony Franz stated under oath that 1) he and Knorr had the final word in translation; 2) he (Franz) was head of the Society's publicity department; and 3) translations and interpretations came from God, invisibly communicated to the publicity department by "angels of various ranks who control[led]" the translators.[5] These statements by the leaders and translators concerning the accuracy of their *New World Translation* is evidence they believe the Watchtower's claim to be God's sole channel on earth.

13

What do recognized Greek scholars believe about the accuracy of the *NWT*?

Greek scholars, both Christian and non-Christian, almost universally reject the *NWT*, calling it biased and inaccurate. Consider some examples. Until his death, Dr. Julius Mantey was one of the leading Greek scholars in the world. He was author of the *Hellenistic Greek Reader* and coauthor, with H.E. Dana, of *A Manual Grammar of the Greek New Testament.* The Watchtower itself cited him as a Greek authority who allegedly supported the accuracy of their translation. However, not only did he reject the *NWT* as biased and inaccurate, he publicly demanded that the Society stop misquoting his *Grammar* to support it (see appendix). Of the *NWT* translation he wrote,

> I have never read any New Testament so badly translated as *The Kingdom Interlinear Translation of the Greek Scriptures.* In fact, it is not their translation at all. Rather,

it is a distortion of the New Testament. The translators used what J.B. Rotherham had translated in 1893, in modern speech, and changed the readings in scores of passages to state what Jehovah's Witnesses believe and teach. That is *distortion*, not translation.[6]

The late Dr. Bruce Metzger, former professor of New Testament language and literature at Princeton Theological Seminary and author of *The Text of the New Testament* (Oxford, 1968), observed, "The Jehovah's Witnesses have incorporated in their translations of the New Testament several quite erroneous renderings of the Greek."[7]

Dr. Robert Countess wrote his dissertation for his PhD in Greek on the *NWT*.* He concluded that the Jehovah's Witnesses' translation

has been sharply unsuccessful in keeping doctrinal considerations from influencing the actual translation. It must be viewed as a radically biased piece of work. At some points it is actually dishonest. At others it is neither modern nor scholarly. And interwoven throughout its fabric is inconsistent application of its own principles enunciated in the Foreword and Appendix.[8]

British scholar H.H. Rowley asserts, "From beginning to end this volume is a shining example of how the Bible should not be translated." He calls it "an insult to the Word of God."[9]

The scholarly community has rendered its verdict on the *NWT*. The Society cannot blame the verdict on alleged Christian bias or "Trinitarian bias," for even non-Christian scholars of New Testament Greek agree that the *NWT* is inaccurate.[10] They have arrived at this

---

* Dr. Countess was a guest on our television program, along with two former leaders from the Watchtower. During the program, he detailed many of the Watchtower's distortions.[11]

conclusion by means of rules of grammar, word meanings, and principles of translation that the Watchtower Society has blatantly violated.

14

What are some examples of *NWT* mistranslation?

The Watchtower Society has warned, "God does not deal with persons who ignore his Word and go according to their own independent ideas." The Watchtower further asserts that Jehovah is against those who "steal" or change words from his Bible to make wrong applications.[12]

Yet the Watchtower has perpetrated just such error by incorporating hundreds of mistranslations in the *NWT*. While space allows us the opportunity to examine only a few examples of its mistranslations, even these few show that the Watchtower Society's claims to publish an honest, unbiased, accurate translation of the Bible are inaccurate and misleading.

In each of the examples below we will a) list both the *New World Translation* (*NWT*) and the New International Version (NIV) translations for comparison, b) give the Watchtower Society's reason for mistranslating, and c) explain why the Jehovah's Witnesses' *New World Translation* is biased and inaccurate.

Illustration 1—Titus 2:13

a) *Comparison of translations of Titus 2:13.* (The same mistranslation occurs in 2 Peter 1:1.) The Jehovah's Witnesses have translated Titus 2:13 in this way:

> *NWT:* "While we wait for the happy hope and glorious manifestation of the great God and of [the] Savior of us,

Christ Jesus." (Jehovah's Witnesses have added the words "of [the]" in front of the word "Savior.")

The NIV translates thus:

NIV: "While we wait for the blessed hope—the glorious appearing of our great God and Savior, Jesus Christ."

b) *The reason the Jehovah's Witnesses have mistranslated this verse is to deny the deity of Jesus Christ, a doctrine they do not accept.*

c) *Proof and documentation from scholars that the* NWT *translators dishonestly translated this verse.*

By adding the words "of [the]," the NWT obscures the fact that in this verse Paul clearly called Jesus "our God and Savior." They have made it read as if Paul were speaking of two persons here, God and Jesus, rather than one, namely Jesus. Paul expressly stated that it is Jesus who is our great God and Savior. The Jehovah's Witnesses completely violate what Greek grammarians call "Granville Sharp's rule" for the use of the article with personal nouns in a series.

In essence, Sharp's rule states that when two singular personal nouns (God and Savior) of the same case (God and Savior are both in the same case in Greek), are connected by *and* (the Greek word is *kai*) and the modifying article *the* (the Greek word is *ho*) appears only before the first noun, not before the second, both nouns must refer to the *same* person.

No other conclusion is possible. In Titus 2:13, "God" and "Savior" are connected by "and." "The" appears only before "God." Therefore, "God" and "Savior" must refer to the same person—Jesus. (The same rule also applies to the words in 2 Peter 1:1 that the NWT has also mistranslated.)

Conclusive facts

Scholars have conclusively shown that in ancient times the phraseology "god and savior" was used of a ruling king, clearly showing that only one person was meant. Moreover, in an exhaustive study, the German theologian C. Kuehne found Sharp's rule to be without a single clear exception in the entire New Testament.[13]

The weight of the evidence and scholarship requires that the words in these verses must be translated "our God and Savior, Jesus Christ," as Dr. Bruce Metzger stated:

> In support of this translation [that "our God and Savior" must refer only to Jesus Christ] there may be quoted such eminent grammarians of the Greek New Testament as P.W. Schmiedel, J.H. Moulton, A.T. Robertson, F. Blass, and A. Debrunner. All of these scholars concur in the judgment that only one person is referred to in Titus 2:13 and that therefore, it must be rendered, "our great God and Savior, Jesus Christ."[14]

Greek scholars Dana and Mantey, in their *Manual Grammar of the Greek New Testament*, confirm Sharp's rule and then explain, "Second Peter 1:1…means that Jesus is our God and Savior. After the same manner Titus 2:13…asserts that Jesus is the great God and Savior." The greatest English-speaking Greek scholar, A.T. Robertson, insisted that "one person, *not* two, is in mind in 2 Peter 1:1,"[15] which must be read, "to those who through the righteousness of our God and Savior Jesus Christ have received a faith as precious as ours."

Even the context of Titus 2:13 shows that one person, not two, was in Paul's mind, for Paul wrote of the "glorious appearing" of that person. The Bible knows of only one such appearing—when "the Son of Man [Jesus]... comes in his glory" (Luke 9:26). Indeed, an appearing of "the invisible God" other than as the visible Christ, who is His image (Colossians 1:15), would be impossible.

From all of this, scholars conclude that the Jehovah's Witnesses' *New World Translation* of Titus 2:13 is a biased and inaccurate translation.

Illustration 2—Colossians 1:17

a) *Comparison of translations of Colossians 1:17.* The Jehovah's Witnesses have translated Colossians 1:17 in this way (everyone agrees this verse speaks of Jesus):

> *NWT:* "Also, he is before all [other] things and by means of him all [other] things were made to exist." (The Jehovah's Witnesses have unnecessarily inserted the word "other" in brackets twice, when this word does not appear at all in the Greek text.)

The NIV translates thus:

> *NIV:* "He is before all things, and in him all things hold together."

b) *The reason the Jehovah's Witnesses have mistranslated this verse is to change the fact that Christ is eternal and therefore God—a doctrine they deny.* To do so, they unnecessarily insert a word not found in the original Greek language, which gives the false impression that Christ himself was a created being and not eternal.

c) *Proof and documentation that the NWT distorts this verse:*

In Colossians 1:17 the Watchtower Society's translators have inserted the word "other" twice, in brackets (which they also did in three more places in verses 16-20). They did this to imply that Christ himself is not the Creator. But as their own Greek interlinear shows,[16] the Greek word *panta* means "all things," *not* "all *other* things" (emphasis added).

What is the reason they give for their misleading translation? The Watchtower claims that inserting "other" five times is justified because the context *implies* it. But if they simply translate only the words in the text of Scripture, nothing at all implies it. The only thing that implies it is their own bias against Christ's deity.

As mentioned, the Watchtower Society's own Greek interlinear version proves embarrassing because it shows there is no "other" in the Greek text. Yet this didn't prevent earlier editions of the *NWT* from inserting "other" *without* parentheses or brackets, implying that it *was* part of the original Greek text (as is seen in the 1950 and 1953 editions). Even the 1965 edition of *Make Sure of All Things* quotes Colossians 1:15-20 in this manner, implying that "other" is actually in the Greek five different times.[17] This is simply not true.

This is not the only place the Jehovah's Witnesses have added words to the text. Recent versions of the *NWT* have inserted the word "other" in Philippians 2:9 to change the meaning of that verse. The meaning about Jesus is changed from "the name that is above every name" to "the name that is above every other name."

The Society's objectivity cannot be more questionable than in examples of this type. The translators have added words to the Bible in order to deny what is clearly taught.

John 8:58—a similar example. This verse is absolute proof that Jesus claimed to be God. Since Jehovah's Witnesses do not believe this, they have deliberately and, again, dishonestly changed the words. Instead of translating Jesus as saying, "before Abraham was born, I am" (NIV), the Jehovah's Witnesses rendered the words, "before Abraham came into existence, I have been" (*NWT*).

Christ's actual statement—that he was the "I am"— was clearly understood by the Jews to mean Jesus had applied to himself the divine name of God used in the Old Testament (Exodus 3:14; Isaiah 43:10). In Exodus, Moses is standing before the burning bush and asks God,

> "Suppose I go to the Israelites and say to them, 'The God of your fathers has sent me to you,' and they ask me, 'What is his name?' Then what shall I tell them?"
>
> God said to Moses, "I AM WHO I AM. This is what you are to say to the Israelites: 'I AM has sent me to you.'"
>
> God also said to Moses, "Say to the Israelites, 'The LORD, the God of your fathers—the God of Abraham, the God of Isaac and the God of Jacob—has sent me to you.' This is my name forever, the name by which I am to be remembered from generation to generation" (Exodus 3:13-15).

In John 8:58, Jesus was claiming to be the "I am" who had brought the Jews' forefathers out of Egypt. That is why the next verse reports that they immediately tried to stone him to death for what they saw as blasphemy (John 8:59).

The Jehovah's Witnesses have incorrectly translated Jesus' words "I am" as "I have been" to obscure the fact that he was making a direct claim to being God. In mis-translating these words, they attempt to teach that Jesus was saying he had existed before as Michael the angel, nothing more. But Michael is not even mentioned in Exodus 3, Isaiah 43, or John 8.

Feeling the pressure from scholars, the Watchtower Society has tried to explain its reason for translating the Greek *ego eimi* ("I am") as "I have been" in John 8:58. They claimed it was because the verb *eimi* was in what they called the "perfect indefinite" tense. Then scholars pointed out to them that there has never been a perfect indefinite tense in Greek and that *eimi*, as any beginner's Greek grammar shows, is the first-person singular, present, active, indicative form of *einai*, "to be."[18] Therefore it *must* be translated "I am," not "I have been."

At that point the Society changed their mind and gave a new reason for mistranslating this verse. Unfortunately, their second answer was also incorrect. Nevertheless, the Watchtower Society still maintains from time to time that *eimi* is in the "perfect indefinite" tense.[19]

At the same time the Society continues to mistranslate "I am" in its English Bible. Only its theological bias can explain its blatant misrepresentation.

A house divided

Interestingly, the Watchtower Society's *Kingdom Interlinear,* which shows the Greek words, actually condemns the *New World Translation,* correctly giving "I am" directly beneath *ego eimi.* But unfortunately, no Jehovah's Witness will ever accept the truth thus shown, because the Society translators further perpetuate their distortion by placing "I have been" in the column to the right—without any grammatical or other justification.[20]

Illustration 3—Matthew 25:46

a) *Comparison of translations of Matthew 25:46.* The Jehovah's Witnesses have translated Matthew 25:46 in this way:

> NWT: "And these will depart into everlasting cutting-off, but the righteous ones into everlasting life."

The NIV translates this verse as follows:

> NIV: "Then they will go away to eternal punishment, but the righteous to eternal life."

b) *The reason Jehovah's Witnesses have mistranslated this verse is to deny the biblical teaching on continuous, eternal punishment, or eternal punishing, and replace it with their doctrine of the annihilation of the wicked.*

c) *Proof and documentation that the* NWT *mistranslates this verse:*

All standard Greek dictionaries define the Greek word in question in Matthew 25:46—*kolasin*—as "punishment," not "cutting-off," as the Jehovah's Witnesses have claimed it means. The Watchtower Society is in conflict with standard Greek authorities,[21] which all note that the word *kolasin* must be translated as "punishment." This definition is clearly substantiated by the word's use during New Testament times. For example, one early Christian writing says that "evil-doers among men receive their reward not among the living only, but also await punishment (*kolasin*) and much torment (*basanon*)."[22] They could hardly suffer "torment" if they were annihilated, as the Watchtower Society believes.

Greek scholar Julius Mantey wrote that he had "found this word in first-century Greek writings in 107 different contexts, and in every one of them, it has the meaning of punishment, and never 'cutting-off.'"[23]

More denial of eternal punishment. Another verse the Society mistranslates to support its rejection of the biblical doctrine of eternal punishment is Hebrews 9:27. The standard way this is understood can be seen from the NIV's translation, which reads, "Just as man is destined to die once, and after that to face judgment..."

Now, notice how the *NWT* adds words *not in the original* to justify the Watchtower's own biased doctrine: "And as it is reserved for men to die once *for all time* [that is, be annihilated], but after this a judgment." The words "for all time" are not in the Greek text, as the Watchtower's own interlinear shows.[24] Read the *NWT* without the added words and the meaning is crystal clear. Dr. Mantey observes, "No honest scholar would attempt to so pervert the word of God."[25] In the Bible, God himself warns all translators, "Do not add to his words, or he will rebuke you and prove you a liar" (Proverbs 30:6).

Further flagrant examples

Space does not permit discussing all of the following verses, but if you consult standard reference works on the New Testament Greek text, they will show you that in each instance the *NWT* has unnecessarily changed the true meaning of the words. There are literally hundreds of examples of these changes:

1. In Acts 20:28, the actual words "Be shepherds of the church of God, which he bought with his own blood" have been mistranslated by the Watchtower Society as "the blood of His own [Son]" to circumvent Christ's deity.

2. In Hebrews 1:8, the proper translation, "Your throne, O God," has been mistranslated by the Watchtower Society to read, "God is your throne," in order to deny Christ's deity.

3. In Colossians 2:9, "For in Christ all the fullness of the deity lives in bodily form," the word "deity" is mistranslated by the Watchtower Society as "divine quality," again in order to deny Christ's deity.

4. In John 1:1, "In the beginning was the Word, and the Word was with God, and the Word was God," the phrase, "the Word was God" is mistranslated by the Watchtower Society as "the Word was a god" to deny Christ's deity.

All of this clearly shows that the Watchtower Society miserably fails to pass the test of accurately translating the Bible. Because the Watchtower's *New World Translation* has universally been condemned as biased and inaccurate, it cannot legitimately claim it is faithfully presenting the Word of God. If it is not faithfully presenting the Word of God, the Watchtower Society cannot possibly be the sole channel on earth through which God has chosen to lead all men.

TEST TWO

If the Watchtower Society is the sole channel for God on earth, then according to the Bible, its prophecies must come true. How reliable have its prophecies been?

Distorting God's Word is serious enough. But making God a liar by speaking false prophecy in his name, so that people will worship a false god, is an offense so serious that in the Old Testament it brought the death penalty (Deuteronomy 13:1-5). Today, according to these verses, the Watchtower stands under the judgment of God.

15

What does the Watchtower Society teach and claim about prophecy?

In the *Watchtower* of March 1, 1975, Jehovah's Witness leaders declared, "The Bible itself establishes the rules for testing a prophecy in Deuteronomy 18:20-23 and 13:1-8." Its own rules, with which we agree, are biblical and are our standard; they demand 100 percent accuracy for any prophecy that is made. The Society's publication *Aid to Bible Understanding* teaches Jehovah's Witnesses that prophecy includes "a declaration of something to come" and that "the source of all true prophecy is Jehovah God." This publication further states that "correct understanding of prophecy would still be made available by God...particularly in the foretold 'time of the end.'"[26] (In context, "time of the end" here includes the emergence of the Watchtower Society.)

Aid to Bible Understanding further defines a "prophet" as "one through whom the divine will and purpose are made known." Further, the Watchtower Society makes the logical claim that it is *the true prophetic mouthpiece for God on earth at this time*.[27] The Watchtower Society tells all Jehovah's Witnesses that "the three essentials for establishing the credentials of the true prophet" are

1. speaking in Jehovah's name,

2. that "the things foretold would come to pass," and

3. that these prophecies would promote true worship by being in harmony with God's already revealed Word.

The Watchtower claims that the true prophet would

"express…God's mind on matters…[and] every prediction [will be] related to God's will, purpose, standards or judgment."[28]

By these lofty claims, the Watchtower Society has succinctly declared both its position and authority. It claims to speak in the name of Jehovah, to be his prophet predicting future events, and to be in harmony with his Word. It confidently predicts that what it says must "come to pass." For example, the September 1, 1979, *Watchtower* declared, "For nearly 60 years now the Jeremiah class [the Jehovah's Witnesses] have *faithfully* spoken forth Jehovah's word."[29]

In the next question, we will examine some of the Watchtower prophecies as well as the implications of the Society's claims to be speaking for God.

16

Has the Watchtower Society ever given false prophecies?

How have the predictions of the Watchtower Society stood the test of history? Let's take a moment to investigate a few of these predictions. The Watchtower Society has frequently attempted to predict the exact date for the start of the Battle of Armageddon and the end of the world. (Unless otherwise noted, all quotations are from the *Watchtower*.)[30]

Would you believe the Jehovah's Witnesses have predicted the end of the world at least 13 times? They said it would end in 1877, 1886, 1914, 1915, 1925, 1939, 1940, 1941, 1942, 1943, 1946, 1950, and 1975!

But the Watchtower not only said these things, they put their prophetic statements about when the world would end in print and left a trail of evidence for all to see.

An unenviable record

In 1982, after a hundred-year string of failed predictions, former Jehovah's Witness leader William Cetnar said, "Now many Jehovah's Witnesses have that new disease called 'lack of memory.' They can't even remember ever saying the world would come to an end."[31]

Let's look at a few predictions the Watchtower has made (in the name of God) concerning the end of the world—what they often call Armageddon. (Because they believe Jesus has already returned invisibly, they look forward to the Battle of Armageddon as "actually one of the best things that could happen to us" because they believe it will usher in "paradise earth," not the second coming of Christ.[32]) As you examine these prophecies, see if you agree that God spoke through them and gave the world the truth. Here are just a few of the predictions they have made through the years:[33]

The early years of Watchtower prophecy

> In 1877: "THE END OF THIS WORLD…is nearer than most men suppose."

> In 1886: "The *time* is come for Messiah to take the dominion of the earth."

> In 1889: "We present proofs that the setting up of the kingdom of God has already begun…and that 'the battle of the great day of God almighty' (Revelation 16:14), which will end in AD 1914 with the complete overthrow of the earth's present rulership, is already commenced."

(In the 1915 edition of the same publication they changed "AD 1914" to "AD 1915.")

On July 15, 1894: "We see no reason for changing the figures—nor could we change them if we would. *They are, we believe, God's dates not ours* (emphasis added). But bear in mind that the end of 1914 is not the date for the *beginning*, but for the *end* of the time of trouble."

In 1904: "The stress of the great time of trouble will be on us soon, somewhere between 1910 and 1912 culminating with the end of the 'times of the Gentiles,' October 1914."

On May 1, 1914: "There is absolutely no ground for Bible students to question that the consummation of this gospel age is now even at the door...The great crisis... that will consume the ecclesiastical heavens and the social earth, is very near."

But the year 1914 ended without a single one of these predictions coming true.

In 1917, Charles Taze Russell, founder and first president of the Jehovah's Witnesses, said of World War I, "The present great war in Europe is the beginning of the Armageddon of the Scriptures."

After Russell's death, Judge Rutherford continued the tradition of failed prophecies given in the name and authority of God. He believed and stated that 1925 would mark the year of Christ's kingdom. He was wrong:

In 1922, in the *Watchtower* magazine: "The date 1925 is even more distinctly indicated by the Scriptures because it is fixed by the law of God to Israel.... [One can see how] even before 1925 the great crisis will be reached and probably passed."

In 1923, the *Watchtower* magazine stated, "Our thought is that 1925 is definitely settled by the Scriptures." But these and all other predictions proved false.

More caution observed

After utterly failing in the 1914 and 1925 predictions and finding that many people were leaving the Society, the leaders of the Watchtower became more cautious in setting dates. Nevertheless, they continued to hold out the promise of the imminency of Armageddon and the subsequent millennial kingdom. From 1930 to 1939 there were numerous declarations made about the future. For example:

In 1930: "The great climax is at hand."

In 1931: "Armageddon is at hand…"

In 1933: "The incontrovertible proof that the time of deliverance is at hand."

In 1933: "That [Jehovah] has now opened these prophecies to the understanding of His anointed is evidence that the time of the battle is near; hence the prophecy is of profound interest to the anointed."

In 1939: "The battle of the great day of God Almighty is very near."

In fact, from May 1940 to April 15, 1943, just three short years, the Society made at least 44 predictions of the imminence of Armageddon. Here are a few examples from this period and later:

In September 1940: "The kingdom is here, the king is enthroned. Armageddon is just ahead…The great climax has been reached."

In the *Watchtower*, September 15, 1941: "The FINAL END IS VERY NEAR"; it also spoke of "the remaining months before Armageddon…"

On January 15, 1942: "The time is at hand for Jesus Christ to take possession of all things."

On May 1, 1942: "Now, with Armageddon immediately before us…"

On May 1, 1943: "The final end of all things…is at hand."

On September 1, 1944: "Armageddon is near at hand."

In 1946: "The disaster of Armageddon…is at the door."

In 1950: "The March is on! Where? To the field of Armageddon for the 'war of the great day of God the Almighty.'"

In 1953: "Armageddon is so near at hand it will strike the generation now living."

In 1955: "It is becoming clear that the war of Armageddon is near its breaking out point."

In 1958: "When will Armageddon be fought?…It will be very soon."

Missing truth

The foregoing are just a few of the many false prophecies the *Watchtower* has made over the years. Is there any wonder the Jehovah's Witness leaders in their October 1968 *Awake!* magazine, were forced to admit that "certain persons" had previously falsely predicted the end of the world? In this article, Jehovah's Witness leaders asked why these false prophecies had been given. Every Jehovah's Witness should take note of what they said. They said it was because they *lacked* God's guidance. The Watchtower leadership admitted,

> True, there have been those in times past who predicted an "end to the world," even announcing a specific date. The "end" did not come. *They were guilty of false prophesying.* Why? What was missing?...Missing from such people were God's truths and the evidence that He was guiding and using them. But what about today? Today we have the evidence required, all of it, and it is overwhelming! (emphasis added).[34]

Notice that the Watchtower leaders have condemned their own divinely inspired predecessors as false prophets. They admit that, all through the years during which these men said they were speaking in the name and authority of God, they were really lying and giving false prophecies.

If we accept that they gave false prophecies, then according to the *New World Translation*, God in Deuteronomy 18:20-22 says,

> However, the prophet who presumes to speak in my name a word that I have not commanded him to speak or who speaks in the name of other gods, that prophet must die. And in case you should say in your heart: "How shall we know the word that Jehovah has not spoken?" When the prophet speaks in the name of Jehovah and the word does not occur or come true, that is the word that Jehovah did not speak. With presumptuousness the prophet spoke it. You must not get frightened at him (*NWT*).

Further embarrassments

In spite of the tragic record of predictions that did not come to pass, the Watchtower leadership disregarded the Word of God in Deuteronomy 18. And, as the above quote from *Awake!* magazine shows, they asked the people to confidently believe they would *now* speak for God in predicting the future. At that point they began to strongly imply it would be the year 1975 in which Armageddon would occur,[35] as listed below:[36]

In 1973: "The 'Great Tribulation' is very near."

Again in 1973: "According to the Bible's time-table, the beginning of the seventh millennium of mankind's existence on earth is near at hand, within this generation."

In May 1974: The world's end was said to be "so very near" that Jehovah's Witnesses were commended who sold "their homes and property" to devote themselves to full-time service in "the short time remaining before the wicked world's end."

In 1975: "The fulfillment…is immediately ahead of us."

Again in 1975: "Very short must be the time that remains."

Many Jehovah's Witnesses living today can remember when the year 1975 came and went, bringing great discouragement to the faithful and providing further embarrassment to the Watchtower Society.

But the charade still continued. From 1976 to 1981 the Society repeatedly said that Armageddon was "very near," "at hand," and made other similar remarks. And from 1981 to the present the Society still claims that the world is near its end. Consider some more recent examples from their Web site, from the years 1992, 2005, and 2006: [37]

> In 1992: "The end of the world is near."

> In 2005: "There is no doubt about it. The end of Satan's system [this world] is close at hand."

> In 2006: "Soon it [this world] will come to its end…and Armageddon is but a short time off."

An untrustworthy source

Jehovah's Witnesses believe that the Watchtower's authoritative statements are true and genuinely reflect God's guidance. But if the Society has been indisputably wrong in every period it has prophesied, how can modern Witnesses trust it?

The exit marked "Failed Prophecy"

Thousands of Jehovah's Witnesses have left the Watchtower after having lived through the high expectations and heartbreaking disappointments of the false prophecies about the world's end. Thousands more have left when they investigated these false prophecies in the Watchtower literature.

The Watchtower Society claims that Jehovah's Witnesses' "unswerving attention to such inspired prophecy has held them true to the right course till now."[38] After reading its false prophecies through the years and its own admission that it lied, what do you think?

The Society still claims of Armageddon that "Jehovah has His own fixed date for its arrival."[39] But the Watchtower has missed that date every time it has predicted it. According to the Bible, God says,

If what a prophet proclaims in the name of the LORD does not take place or come true, that is a message the LORD has not spoken. That prophet has spoken presumptuously. Do not be afraid of him (Deuteronomy 18:22).

17

Is the Watchtower Society hypocritical?

Jehovah's Witnesses have admitted serious errors. In 1975, in an official Watchtower publication, *Man's Salvation*, they now admit that Charles Taze Russell was wrong in his 1874 prediction of Christ's Second Coming.[40] They admit that they were wrong in their 1914 prediction. They admit that they were wrong in their prediction of 1925. They admit that they were wrong about their prediction in 1975.[41]

Yet that same year, in their *1975 Yearbook*, the Society claims that *for over a century* "Jehovah's servants" have "enjoyed spiritual enlightenment and direction."[42] Doesn't this appear contradictory? Does the evidence show they have passed the second test they themselves laid down, that any prophecy given in the name of God must come true? Have their prophecies come true 100 percent of the time?[43] Have they come true 1 percent of the time? If not, can the Watchtower Society legitimately claim it is God's sole channel of communication to men on earth today?

TEST THREE

If the Watchtower Society is God's sole channel for communication on earth, then its scholarship should be trustworthy—but is it?

18

Has the Watchtower Society ever lied, covered up, or changed important doctrines, dates, and Bible interpretations?

If God actually speaks to all people through the Watchtower Society—giving prophecy, Bible interpretations, and other instruction—from the Watchtower materials it appears he must change his mind a great deal. These words and our question above sound blunt, but we are only doing what Judge Rutherford told us to do for the Jehovah's Witnesses:

> If the message Jehovah's Witnesses are bringing to the people is true, then it is of greatest importance to mankind. If it is false, then it is the duty of the clergymen and others who support them to come boldly forward and plainly tell the people wherein the message is false.[44]

The fact is, the Watchtower Society's leaders have at times lied and covered up important material. Even the *Watchtower*, in a 1960 issue, encourages "hiding the truth from God's enemies." They say it is proper to deceive people (God's enemies) but they claim this is not lying. This is because they have a different definition of lying, as stated in *Aid to Bible Understanding*, where they say that lying "generally involves saying something false to a person who is *entitled* to know the truth."[45] The fact is, however, it is not just "God's enemies" they have lied to, but their own dedicated members.

Altered dates and prophecies

Here are a few of the changes in dates and prophecies that the Watchtower Society has made through the years. What is so condemning is that all of this can be found in its own allegedly authoritative writings. For example:

1. The Watchtower Society changed the beginning of the "time of the end" from the date 1799 to 1914;

2. it changed the second coming of Christ from the date 1874 to 1914;

3. it changed the entire nature of the second coming of Christ from an earthly and visible return to a heavenly and invisible return;

4. it changed the time of the "first resurrection" from the date 1878 to 1914; and

5. it changed the date of the termination of the 6,000 years of creation from the year 1872 to 1972 and then once again to 1975.[46]

Why so many changes? Simple: The predicted events didn't happen. The changes were made to cover up its failed prophecies and hide the fact that God really hadn't spoken through the Society.

Altered doctrines and interpretations

As mentioned, the Watchtower Society has also made changes concerning important doctrines. Among the most notable, the Society

1. changed its doctrine concerning life-saving

vaccination from commands rejecting it to permission to accept it.

2. changed the identity of the "Faithful and Wise
   Servant" from Charles Taze Russell, its first president, to the Watchtower Society itself.

3. once said the book of Ruth should be interpreted
   as history, but later changed and said it should be
   read as prophecy.

4. changed the identity of "Abaddon" in Revelation
   9:11, first saying this angel was Satan, and later
   saying this was Jesus Christ.

5. in its early years accepted blood transfusions, but
   then later made rejection of blood transfusions a
   key doctrine.

6. first accepted the worship of Jesus, but now rejects
   the worship of Jesus.

7. changed the doctrine concerning the resurrection
   of the dead—first *all* were to be raised, now only
   some were to be raised.

8. changed its view of Israel—from literal (a physical
   nation) to spiritual (all believers).

9. changed the definition of the "superior authorities," found in Romans 13 (*NWT*), from political
   rulers on earth to God and Jesus in heaven, and
   then back again to political rulers on earth.[47]

These changes and many more, force people to ask,
"Can the average Jehovah's Witness know that what
he or she is told is true today won't be declared false
tomorrow?" Former Jehovah's Witness and current

professor Edmond Gruss, in his standard text *Apostles of Denial*, declares that "thousands of reinterpretations of Scripture" and many new doctrinal points were developed after C.T. Russell's death; Gruss cites many illustrations. Former Witness William J. Schnell notes, "I had observed *The Watchtower* magazine change our doctrines between 1917 and 1928 no less than 148 times."[48] One example is Luke 16:19-31, which has been interpreted in five different ways.[49] How, then, can the average Jehovah's Witness know God's true mind on any passage of Scripture?[50] Worse, how can even God know his own mind?

These are only a small sample of the changes the Watchtower Society has made in the name of God concerning its Bible interpretation, its doctrine, and its prophetic dates. Do its statements support the claim that the Watchtower Society "from the time of its organization until now" has been God's sole "collective channel for the flow of biblical truth to men on earth"? Do its false prophecies support the claim that for over a century Jehovah's servants have "enjoyed spiritual enlightenment and direction"? Again, it raises the question of how the Watchtower Society could say "Jehovah never makes any mistakes,"[51] when it also claims Jehovah is speaking through it.

In the Bible, God himself clearly states he is the "God of truth" who "cannot lie" (Psalm 31:5; Titus 1:2 NASB). In fact, "it is impossible for God to lie" for "no lie is of the truth" (Hebrews 6:18; 1 John 2:21 NASB). God does not make mistakes concerning dates, nor does he change his mind on doctrinal matters. Is there any other conclusion we can come to except that the Watchtower Society has misled millions of people in claiming it alone is God's sole channel of communication on earth today?

TEST FOUR

If the Watchtower Society admits it received many of its teachings from angels or spirits and those teachings have proven to be false, is such a source trustworthy?

19

Has the Watchtower Society ever claimed to receive information from angels or spirits?

It can be documented that leaders in the Watchtower Society dabbled in the occult in its early years.[52] However, the Watchtower Society's official position toward occult activity is supposedly in agreement with the prohibition found in Deuteronomy 18:9-12. Nevertheless, today the Watchtower Society appears to be unsuspectingly involved in the occult in at least one manner: It seems to accept demonic guidance and revelations, which may come to it in the disguise of angelic or spiritistic contacts.

What kind of angels?

The Watchtower has historically claimed "angelic guidance" for its Bible translators in their work on the *NWT* and also in their writing of Jehovah's Witnesses' doctrine and practice. If real supernatural activity has occurred, and the Watchtower's translation, doctrines, and practices have failed to meet biblical, moral,[53] and scholarly standards, it is impossible that the supernatural assistance was from God. Godly angels would never lend help to an organization that denies the true nature of who God is, deliberately distorts his Word, and completely rejects his Son. But the Bible says that fallen angels—also called demons—would. The Bible further declares that Satan, the greatest fallen angel, masquerades as an "angel of light" while doing so (see 2 Corinthians 11:14-15).

An uncomfortable kinship

Besides the Watchtower Society's express claim (see page 42) that "angels" guided its translators in their work on the *New World Translation,* William Cetnar, former service department member in the Jehovah's Witnesses headquarters at Brooklyn, New York, found many Watchtower beliefs were also professed by a spirit-possessed medium the Society was quoting.[54]

Judge Rutherford indicated that an angel or angels helped write the *Watchtower* magazine when he said, for example, "The Lord through His angel sees to it that the information is given to His people in due time." F.W. Franz also spoke of angels guiding the Watchtower. He said, "We believe that the angels of God are used in directing Jehovah's Witnesses."[55]

Among other things, the Watchtower Society claims that angels enlighten and comfort, bring refreshing truths, and transmit information to "God's anointed people." The *Watchtower* magazine makes another statement of the belief that angels guide the leaders of Jehovah's Witnesses: "Jehovah's Witnesses today make their declaration of the good news of the kingdom under angelic direction and support."[56]

God's channel?

Additional related declarations are found in the *Watchtower* magazine. In 1981 and 1960, the leaders of the Jehovah's Witnesses claimed to be God's "channel of communication," actively "channeling" (the use of this common New Age term is theirs) since the days of

Rutherford. In a 1972 issue, they claimed that all spiritual direction is supplied by invisible angels. In 1933, 1935, and 1987, they claimed that the name "Jehovah's Witnesses" and their key doctrine of "Christ's" invisible return in 1914 were channeled by invisible angels.[57]

Under their second president, J.F. Rutherford, the Jehovah's Witnesses received most of their basic doctrines. Yet Rutherford believed that God's "holy spirit" (which he taught was God's impersonal active force) had ceased to function as his teacher and had been replaced by angels, who taught him in his mind.[58] Today, the Society, perhaps embarrassed by exposés, may deny it receives angelic revelations, but one cannot deny the Watchtower Society claim to have received them for some five decades, neither can one but suspect the denial. One denial was published in 1993: "[Jehovah's Witnesses] today do not have angelic revelations or divine inspiration."[59]

Yet claims for angelic guidance in 2008 can be found on their Web site, for example: "Jehovah uses them to assist and protect his loyal servants on earth" and "Angels deliver God's messages."[60] Today the Society's leaders claim that both "holy spirit" and "angels" communicate information to them.[61]

In conclusion, these startling admissions from the Watchtower documenting that it receives information and guidance from supernatural sources (that is, "angels")—coupled with all its false prophecies, biased Bible translation, and unbiblical teachings—lead us to believe the Society is receiving its information from lying spirits the Bible identifies as demons, rather than from God.

As the apostle Paul warned us,

Such men are false apostles, deceitful workmen, masquerading as apostles of Christ. And no wonder, for Satan himself masquerades as an angel of light. It is not surprising, then, if his servants masquerade as servants of righteousness. Their end will be what their actions deserve (2 Corinthians 11:13-15).

Conclusion

20

What can you do if you are a Jehovah's Witness who desires to live for God and Christ and yet are unsure about what you have been taught?

First, if you are a Jehovah's Witness, don't be discouraged. Please don't give up on God because someone has misled you. Perhaps you accepted the Watchtower's claims without first testing them carefully. In a pluralistic age, discerning God's truth is a spiritual battle. It's not easy. But possibly your own doubts and discouragement will become the very means by which God leads you into the truth and into a personal relationship with him.

Think about how wonderful it would be if you didn't have to earn your salvation by going door-to-door and performing a myriad of other works. Think about being truly forgiven—fully and forever—and becoming a child of God himself, where God lives in your life and empowers you and promises to take you to heaven when you die.

Second, realize you aren't alone. Former Worldwide Governing Body board member Raymond Franz estimates that between 1970 and 1979 over 750,000 Jehovah's Witnesses were disfellowshipped or left the Watchtower organization.[1] Many of them are willing to encourage you through information, e-mail, conferences, or personal visits (for example, see TowerWatch.org). They know what you are going through and want to help you.

Third, take the initiative to learn the truth for yourself. The Watchtower has told you before that "sincere seekers for the truth want to know what is right."[2] If you study the Bible on your own, in humility before God, God says he himself will show you the truth:

> If any of you lacks wisdom, let him ask of God, who gives to all men generously and without reproach, and it will be given to Him. Draw near to God and He will draw near to you (James 1:5; 4:8 NASB).

This is not an idle promise. Christians from across the world can testify to the powerful testimony of Scripture. God himself will help you find the answers and understand his Word. It will happen in your life. Ask him, and he'll help you. Believe and obey his Word—don't alter it—and you will know the truth and, as Jesus promised, "the truth will make you free" (John 8:31-32 NASB).

Fourth, accept God's loving and free gift of salvation in Christ Jesus. (Again, the reason God's grace is so amazing is because no works are needed to earn it!) God never intended for you to spend your life in a hopeless, never-ending attempt to earn your own salvation by measuring up to his or any other standard of perfection. He has already told us it's impossible for any person to do so. He provides the perfect righteousness we need when we trust Christ to be our sin-bearer, the one who paid for all of our sins when he died on the cross. God ascribes Christ's perfect track record of righteousness to you the moment you trust Jesus to be your Savior.

Because of your fallen nature, you'll never be able to do it (see Romans 8:3), "but because of His great love for us, God, who is rich in mercy, made us alive with Christ even when we were dead in transgressions—it is by grace you have been saved" (Ephesians 2:4-5).

Romans 4:5 tells us, "To the man who does not work but trusts God who justifies the wicked, his faith is credited as righteousness."

The really good news that God gives to all of us is…

> There is now no condemnation for those who are in Christ Jesus (Romans 8:1).

> You see, at just the right time, when we were still powerless, Christ died for the ungodly (Romans 5:6).

> The gift of God is eternal life in Christ Jesus our Lord (Romans 6:23).

> We, too, have put our faith in Christ Jesus that we may be justified by faith in Christ and not by observing the law, because by observing the law no one will be justified…I do not set aside the grace of God, for if righteousness could be gained through the law, Christ died for nothing! (Galatians 2:16,21).

Fifth, God wants you to confess your sins and accept his forgiveness, which he provided through Christ's shed blood. Read Isaiah 55:1-3 and see how eagerly God longs for you to come to him to rest. Do you long for eternal life? Do you long for God's total acceptance and love? God's Word says you can *know* you have it:

> The one who believes in the Son of God has the testimony in himself; the one who does not believe God has made him a liar, because he has not believed in the

testimony that God has given concerning his Son. And the testimony is this, that God has *given* us eternal life, and this life is in His Son. *He who has the Son has the life;* he who does not have the Son of God *does not* have the life.

These things I have written to you who believe in the name of the Son of God, so that *you may know that you have eternal life* (1 John 5:10-13 NASB).

A powerful example is found in the scene of Jesus on the cross. He was crucified between two criminals who were sentenced to death for their crimes. One of the men mocked Jesus and told him to get himself down from the cross if he was really God's Son, the Messiah.

The other man, however, had a more humble attitude. He understood he would soon die. He knew Jesus claimed to be God's Son. So he made a request. His solitary wish can be found in one sentence in the Gospel of Luke: "Jesus, remember me when you come into your kingdom" (Luke 23:42).

Just one thing is needed

Getting to heaven does not require a passport, a certain sum of money, or a spectacular level of achievement. It only requires Jesus.

How did Jesus respond? We are told that Jesus answered, "I tell you the truth, today you will be with me in paradise" (Luke 23:43).

That was it. This dying criminal had no time to change his habits, give to the poor, go door-to-door, or even be baptized. He could only ask Jesus to take him into his kingdom, which Jesus called paradise. That's exactly what heaven is.

You can receive the gift of salvation, and know that you have eternal life, right now, by sincerely praying in this way:

> *Dear Jesus, I'm confused. But I long to know you and serve you as you really are. Please reveal who you are to me. I confess that I'm a sinner and incapable of earning favor in your eyes. I believe your words, "You must be born again." I now trust Jesus Christ to be my sin-bearer, my Savior, and my Lord. I receive you into my life, Jesus. I commit myself to you and to your Word. Spiritually, I am putting my faith in you to make me born again right now. From this moment on, I will trust your promise that you will take me to heaven to live with you for all eternity when I die. Thank you for your many promises that give me confidence of what you have now done, and will do, in my life. Amen.*

Romans 10:13 says, "Everyone who calls on the name of the Lord will be saved." "Everyone" means *anyone*. It means you if you just said that prayer. Calling on the name of the Lord is simply praying to Jesus. Notice what happens—you "will be saved." Not maybe, not someday, not "I hope so"—but you "will be saved."

John 1:12 says, "To all who received him, to those who believed in his name, he gave the right to become children of God." This is what God promises he will do for you. Have you called to him?

APPENDIX

What did one prominent Greek scholar say about the Watchtower Society's use of his writings?

"I haven't read any translation that is as diabolical and as damnable as the JW so-called translation... They (the Watchtower Society) hate Jesus Christ."

—DR. JULIUS MANTEY,
"DISTORTIONS OF THE NEW TESTAMENT"[3]

Letter dated July 11, 1974, from Dr. Julius Mantey[*]

Watchtower Bible & Tract Society
117 Adams St.
Brooklyn, New York 11201

Dear Sirs:

I have a copy of your letter addressed to CARIS in Santa Ana, California, and I am writing to express my disagreement with statements made in that letter, as well as in quotations you have made from the Dana-Mantey Greek Grammar.

(1) Your statement: "their work allows for the rendering found in the *Kingdom Interlinear Translation of the Greek Scriptures* at John 1:1." There is no statement in our grammar that was ever meant to imply that "a god" was a permissible translation in John 1:1.

    A. We had no "rule" to argue in support of the trinity.

---

[*] Dr. Julius Mantey, DD, PhD, studied Greek for more than 65 years, was professor of New Testament at Northern Baptist Seminary, Chicago, the author of *A Hellenistic Greek Reader,* and coauthor of the standard intermediate Greek grammar *A Manual Grammar of the Greek New Testament.*

B. Neither did we state that we did have such intention. We were simply delineating the facts inherent in Biblical language.

C. Your quotation from p. 148 (3) was in a paragraph under the heading: "*With the Subject in a Copulative sentence.*" Two examples occur there to illustrate that "the article points out the subject in these examples." But we made no statement in this paragraph about the predicate except that, "as it stands the other persons of the trinity may be implied in *theos.*" And isn't that the opposite of what your translation "a god" infers? You quoted me out of context. On pages 139 and 149 (VI) in our grammar we stated: "without the article *theos* signifies divine essence...*theos en ho logos* emphasizes Christ's participation in the essence of the divine nature." Our interpretation is in agreement with that in NEB and the TEV: "What God was, the Word was"; and with that of Barclay: "The nature of the Word was the same as the nature of God," which you quoted in your letter to CARIS.

(2) Since Colwell's and Harner's articles in *JBL* *[Journal of Biblical Literature]*, especially that of Harner, it is neither scholarly nor reasonable to translate John 1:1 "The Word was a god." Word order has made obsolete and incorrect such a rendering.

(3) Your quotation of Colwell's rule is inadequate because it quotes only a part of his findings. You did not quote this strong assertion: "A predicate nominative which precedes the verb cannot be translated as an indefinite or a 'qualitative' noun solely because of the absence of the article."

(4) Prof. Harner, vol. 92:1 (1973) in *JBL*, has gone beyond Colwell's research and has discovered that anarthrous predicate nouns preceding the verb function

primarily to express the nature or character of the subject. He found this true in 53 passages in the Gospel of John and 8 in the Gospel of Mark. Both scholars wrote that when indefiniteness was intended the gospel writers regularly placed the predicate noun after the verb, and both Colwell and Harner have stated that *theos* in John 1:1 is not indefinite and should not be translated "a god." Watchtower writers appear to be the only ones advocating such a translation now. The evidence appears to be 99% against them.

(5) Your statement in your letter that the sacred text itself should guide one and "not just someone's rule book." We agree with you. But our study proves that Jehovah's Witnesses do the opposite of that whenever the "sacred text" differs with their heretical beliefs. For example the translation of *kolasis* as *"cutting off"* when punishment is the only meaning cited in the lexicons for it. The mistranslation of *ego eimi* as "I have been" in John 8:58. The addition of "for all time" in Heb. 9:27 when nothing in the Greek New Testament supports it. The attempt to belittle Christ by mistranslating *arche tes ktiseos* "beginning of the creation" when he is magnified as "the creator of all things" (John 1:2) and as "equal with God" (Phil. 2:6) before he humbled himself and lived in a human body here on earth. Your quotation of "The Father is greater than I am" (John 14:28) to prove that Jesus was not equal to God overlooks the fact stated in Phil. 2:6-8, when Jesus said that he was still in his voluntary state of humiliation. That state ended when he ascended to heaven. Why the attempt to deliberately deceive people by mispunctuation by placing a comma after "today" in Luke 23:43 when in the Greek, Latin, German and all English translations except yours, *even in the Greek in your KIT,* the comma

occurs after *lego* (I say)—"Today you will be with me in Paradise." Also 2 Cor. 5:8, "to be out of the body and at home with the Lord." These passages teach that the redeemed go immediately to heaven after death, which does not agree with your teachings that death ends all life until the resurrection. Cf. Ps. 23:6 and Heb. 1:10.

The above are only a few examples of Watchtower mistranslations and perversions of God's Word.

In view of the preceding facts, especially because you have been quoting me out of context, I herewith request you not to quote the *Manual Grammar of the Greek New Testament* again, which you have been doing for 24 years. Also that you not quote it or me in any of your publications from this time on.

Also that you publicly and immediately apologize in the *Watchtower* magazine, since my words had no relevance to the absence of the article before *theos* in John 1:1. And please write to CARIS and state that you misused and misquoted my "rule."

On the page before the *Preface* in the grammar are these words: "All rights reserved—no part of this book may be reproduced in any form without permission in writing from the publisher."

If you have such permission, please send me a photocopy of it. If you do not heed these requests you will suffer the consequences.

Regretfully yours,
Julius R. Mantey

RECOMMENDED RESOURCES

Books

Jerry Bergman, *Jehovah's Witnesses: A Comprehensive and Selectively Annotated Bibliography* (Westport, CT: Greenwood Press, 1999).

Robert M. Bowman Jr., *Jehovah's Witnesses* (Grand Rapids, MI: Zondervan Publishing House, 1995).

Robert H. Countess, *The Jehovah's Witnesses' New Testament* (Phillipsburg, NJ: P&R, 1982).

Raymond Franz, *Crisis of Conscience* (Atlanta: Commentary Press, 2002).

Raymond Franz, *In Search of Christian Freedom* (Atlanta: Commentary Press, 1992).

Edmond Gruss, *Apostles of Denial* (Grand Rapids, MI: Baker Books, 1976).

Wilbur Lingle, *Approaching Jehovah's Witnesses in Love: How to Witness Effectively Without Arguing* (Fort Washington, PA: Christian Literature Crusade, 1995).

David A. Reed, *Answering Jehovah's Witnesses: Subject by Subject* (Grand Rapids, MI: Baker Books, 1996).

Ron Rhodes, *The 10 Most Important Things You Can Say to a Jehovah's Witness* (Eugene, OR: Harvest House Publishers, 2001).

Randall Watters, *Thus Saith Jehovah's Witnesses: 120 Years of Revealing Documents from the Watchtower Bible & Tract Society* (available from Freeminds.org).

Web sites

Aomin.org/Witnesses.html

ApologeticsIndex.org

Disfellowshipped.org

Exjws.net

Freeminds.org

Geocities.com/osarsif/index2.htm ("Research on the Watchtower")

Jehovahs-Witness.com

JohnAnkerberg.org

TowerWatch.org

WatchtowerInformationService.org

WitnessInc.org

NOTES

Note: Most Jehovah's Witnesses' materials are published anonymously by the Watchtower Bible and Tract Society (WBTS), Brooklyn, NY. Few are listed with a specific author.

Section One: Introduction

1. Edmond Gruss, *Apostles of Denial: An Examination and Exposé of the History, Doctrines and Claims of the Jehovah's Witnesses* (Grand Rapids, MI: Baker, 1972), pp. 14-16.

2. "Membership and Publishing Statistics," Jehovah's Witnesses official Web site, August 2006. Accessed at www.jw-media.org/people/statistics.htm.

3. Clayton J. Woodworth and George H. Fisher, comp. and ed., Charles Taze Russell, *The Finished Mystery*, vol. 7 of *Studies in the Scriptures*, 1918 ed. (Brooklyn, NY: International Bible Students Assoc., 1917), p. 387; cited in Gruss, *Apostles of Denial*, p. 21.

4. Technically, vol. 7, *The Finished Mystery*, was posthumously compiled and edited by George H. Fisher and Clayton J. Woodworth.

5. *Watchtower*, Sept. 15, 1910, p. 298, from Chicago Bible Students, *Reprints of the Original Watchtower and Herald of Christ's Presence*, 12 volumes plus index (Chicago, IL: Chicago Bible Students), n.d.

6. *Watchtower*, Aug. 15, 1981, pp. 28-29.

7. Lehman was a 17-year Theocratic Ministry School Overseer and 20-year congregation elder. See his Web site, www.towerwatch.org.

8. See Gruss, chapter 5.

9. Gruss, p. 76.

10. Raymond Franz, *Crisis of Conscience* (Atlanta, GA: Commentary, 1983), pp. 345, 347, 354, 290-91, 303, 25-26, 51, 137-39, 147-48, 164-223, 910, 16, 41, 47, 238-39, 344, 52-65, 195, 29-52.

11. Franz, pp. 97, 245, 257.

Section Two: The Worldview of the Jehovah's Witnesses—Practices and Teachings

1. *Life Everlasting in the Freedom of the Sons of God* (WBTS, 1966), p. 181.

2. Edmond Gruss, *We Left Jehovah's Witnesses—A Non-Prophet Organization* (Nutley, NJ: Presbyterian & Reformed, 1974), p. 78.

3. *Watchtower*, Mar. 1, 1979, p. 16.

4. *Watchtower*, Jul. 15, 1960, p. 439, cited in Michael Van Buskirk, *The Scholastic Dishonesty of the Watchtower* (Santa Ana, CA: CARIS, 1976), p. 26.

5. H. Montague, "Watchtower Congregations: Communion or Conflict?" (Costa Mesa, CA: CARIS), p. 7. See Duane Magnani, *The Watchtower Files: Dialogue with a Jehovah's Witness* (Minneapolis: Bethany Fellowship, 1985), p. 17, for documentation from court records of a statement by Nathan H. Knorr that the *Watchtower* is the word of God "without any qualification whatsoever."

6. Gruss, p. 41.

7. *Watchtower*, Feb. 15, 1983, p. 12.

8. *You Can Live Forever in Paradise on Earth* (WBTS, 1982), p. 212.

9. *Blood, Medicine and the Law of God* (WBTS, 1961), p. 55. Cited in Duane Magnani and Arthur Barrett, *Dialogue with Jehovah's Witnesses*, two volumes (Witness, Inc., PO Box 597, Clayton, CA, 1983), vol. 2, p. 371.

10. William and Joan Cetnar, *Questions for Jehovah's Witnesses* (William J. Cetnar: RD #3, Kunkletown, PA, 1983), p. 26; Magnani and Barrett, *Dialogue*, vol. 2, pp. 368-74. For a refutation of this view, see Jerry Bergman, *Jehovah's Witnesses and Blood Transfusions* (St. Louis, MO: Personal Freedom Outreach), n.d.; Walter R. Martin, *Jehovah of the Watchtower* (Chicago: Moody Press, rev. ed. 1974), pp. 91-105.

11. For example, see the *Watchtower*, June 15, 2000; for the official view, see www .watchtower.org/library/hb/index.htm.

12. Dr. Havor Montague, *Jehovah's Witnesses and Blood Transfusions* (Milwaukee: CARIS, 1979).

13. *Man's Salvation Out of World Distress at Hand!* (WBTS, 1975), p. 335; *Watchtower*, Sept. 1, 1979, p. 21; J.F. Rutherford, *Preparation* (WBTS, 1933), pp. 19-20; J.F. Rutherford, *Religion* (WBTS, 1940), p. 104, cited in Edmond Gruss, *Apostles of Denial* (Grand Rapids, MI: Baker, 1972), p. 63; *Watchtower*, Sept. 1, 1979, p. 8.

14. *Watchtower*, Oct. 1, 1952, pp. 596-604. Cited in Walter R. Martin, *Jehovah of the Watchtower*, p. 109.

Section Three: The Theology of the Jehovah's Witnesses

1. C.T. Russell, *Studies in the Scriptures*, vol. 7: *The Finished Mystery*, p. 410. Cited in W.M. Nelson and R.K. Smith, "Jehovah's Witnesses, Part 2, Their Mission," in David Hesselgrave, ed., *Dynamic Religious Movements: Case Studies of Rapidly Growing Religious Movements Around the World* (Grand Rapids, MI: Baker, 1978), p. 181.

2. *Aid to Bible Understanding* (WBTS, 1971), p. 665; Duane Magnani, *The Heavenly Weatherman* (Clayton, CA: Witness, Inc., 1987), pp. 1-8, 42-50, 246-51.

3. *Then Is Finished the Mystery of God* (WBTS, 1969), p. 10; J.F. Rutherford, *Uncovered* (WBTS, 1937), pp. 48-49, cited in Charles S. Braden, *These Also Believe: A Study of Modern American Cults and Minority Religious Movements* (New York: Macmillan, 1970), p. 371. *Let God Be True* (WBTS, 1976), p. 82, states, "Satan is the originator of the 'Trinity' doctrine."

4. *Let God Be True* (WBTS, 1946), p. 83; *Things in Which It Is Impossible for God to Lie* (WBTS, 1965), p. 259; *Watchtower*, Jul. 1982, pp. 2-3.

5. The verses listed with each of these five points should be read in a good modern translation like the New International Version or the New American Standard Bible because some were mistranslated in the King James version and in the NWT. See questions 13 & 14.

6. For an in-depth study of the historical development of the doctrine of the Trinity from apostolic times through the final form of the Nicene Creed adopted at the Council of Constantinople in AD 381, including a line-by-line comparison of the Creed with New Testament teaching, see E. Calvin Beisner, *God in Three Persons* (Wheaton, IL: Tyndale House, 1984).

7. *Is This Life All There Is?* (WBTS, 1974), p. 99.

8. C.T. Russell, *Studies in the Scriptures*, vol. 5, *The Atonement Between God and Man* (East Rutherford, NJ: Dawn Bible Students Assoc., reprint of 1899 ed., n.d.), p. 60.

9. Walter Martin, in "Interview with Dr. Walter Martin on Cults," *The John Ankerberg Show*, 1984.

10. *Aid to Bible Understanding*, (WBTS, 1971), p. 1152; *The Watchtower*, Aug. 22, 1976, pp. 25-26; *Aid to Bible Understanding*, p. 918.

11. *Let God Be True* (WBTS, 1946), p. 65; *Watchtower*, Aug. 15, 1976, p. 495 (compare *Watchtower*, May 15, 1932, p. 155; Nov. 1, 1919, p. 332-33).

12. Russell, *Studies in the Scriptures*, vol. 5, p. 454. Compare note 13 below.

13. *The Truth Shall Make You Free* (WBTS, 1943), p. 264; Anthony Hoekema, *The Four Major Cults* (Grand Rapids, MI: Eerdmans, 1970), p. 272; James Bjornstad, *Counterfeits at Your Door* (Glendale, CA: Regal, 1979), pp. 67-68, 92-94; Nelson and Smith in Hesselgrave, pp. 178-79; *Things in Which It Is Impossible for God to Lie*, p. 219; *Let Your Name Be Sanctified* (WBTS, 1961), p. 272; *Man's Salvation Out of World Distress at Hand!* (WBTS, 1975), pp. 42-43; *Watchtower*, Jan. 15, 1980, p. 31; *Make Sure of All Things, Hold Fast to What Is Fine* (WBTS, 1965), p. 255.

14. *Reasoning from the Scriptures* (WBTS, 1985), pp. 95-98. However, in *Studies in the Scriptures*, vol. 4, *The Battle of Armageddon* (Brooklyn, NY: International Bible Students Assoc., 1917), p. 621, Russell wrote, "Our Lord, the appointed King, is now present, since Oct. 1874, A.D., according to the testimony of the prophets, to those who have ears to hear it."

15. See *Aid to Bible Understanding*, p. 437 and the discussion in Hoekema, pp. 279-85.

16. *Reasoning from the Scriptures*, pp. 76-77.

17. *You May Survive Armageddon into God's New World* (WBTS, 1955), p. 356.

18. The Witnesses may in places define God's grace properly, but they do not live as if it were true. See Edmond Gruss, *We Left Jehovah's Witnesses—a Non-Prophet Organization* (Nutley, NJ: Presbyterian & Reformed, 1974) pp. 131-32; Duane Magnani, *The Watchtower Files* (Minneapolis: Bethany Fellowship, 1985), chapter 13.

19. *Making Your Family Life Happy* (WBTS, 1978), pp. 182-83.

20. *Watchtower*, May 1, 1979, p. 20; compare *Watchtower*, May 1, 1980, p. 13; also Aug. 1, 1981, p. 20.

21. *Life Everlasting in the Freedom of the Sons of God* (WRBS, 1966), p. 400. *Aid to Bible Understanding*, p. 437; *You May Survive Armageddon into God's New World*, pp. 356-57; Gruss, pp. 131-32.

Section Four: Analysis and Critique—"Does God Speak Only Through the Watchtower Society?" Four Tests Examining This Claim

1. Discussions with members and former members; *Reasoning from the Scriptures*, (WBTS, 1985), p. 277.

2. *All Scripture Is Inspired by God and Beneficial* (WBTS, 1963), pp. 326, 327, 30.

3. *The New World Translation of the Holy Scriptures* (WBTS, 1961), p. 5.

4. *The Kingdom Interlinear Translation of the Greek Scriptures* (WBTS, 1969), p. 5. *Reasoning from the Scriptures*, p. 277, states: "We have not used any scholar's

name for reference or recommendations because…the translation must be appraised on its own merits."

5. Cited in Edmond Gruss, *Apostles of Denial* (Grand Rapids, MI: Baker, 1972), pp. 32-33, 219; Gruss has seen the original court transcripts himself. This is a startling admission by Franz, for the control of men by spirits sounds more like demonism than divine inspiration. As a key example, one mediumistic translator of the Bible, who claimed his translation originated in the spirit world, handled several passages similarly to how the Society handles them. The 1937 New Testament translation by occult medium Johannes Greber translates John 1:1, Hebrews 1:8, and other passages the way the *NWT* does. Indeed, the Society quotes Greber's translation to support its own (see note 50 below). If indeed translators were "controlled by angels of various ranks," it was by *unholy* angels—demons. Only they would have so twisted the translation. For documentation as to parallels between the *NWT* and this mediumistic translation, see William and Joan Cetnar, *Questions for Jehovah's Witnesses* (William J. Cetnar, RD #3, Kunkletown, PA, 1983), pp. 48-55.

6. Julius Mantey, *Depth Exploration in the New Testament* (NY: Vantage Press, 1980), pp. 136-37.

7. Bruce M. Metzger, "The Jehovah's Witnesses and Jesus Christ: A Biblical and Theological Appraisal," reprint of *Theology Today* article, Apr. 1953 (Princeton, NJ: Theological Book Agency), p. 74.

8. Dr. Robert Countess, *The Jehovah's Witnesses' New Testament: A Critical Analysis of the New World Translation of the Christian Greek Scriptures* (Phillipsburg, NJ: Presbyterian & Reformed, 1987), pp. 91, 93.

9. H.H. Rowley, "How Not to Translate the Bible," *The Expository Times*, Nov. 1953, pp. 41-42; compare Jan. 1956, cited by Gruss, *Apostles of Denial*, pp. 212-13.

10. For example, see www.foranswer.org/Top_JW/Scholars%20%20NWT.htm; www.reachouttrust.org/articles/jw/jwnwt.htm; www.freeminds.org/doctrine/nwt .htm.

11. Dr. Robert Countess, in "How to Witness to a Jehovah's Witness," *The John Ankerberg Show*, 1983.

12. *Watchtower*, Mar. 15, 1972, p. 189; *Watchtower*, Sept. 1, 1979, p. 30.

13. A.T. Robertson, *A Grammar of the Greek New Testament in the Light of Historical Research* (Nashville, TN: Broadman Press, 1934), p. 786; C. Kuehne, "The Greek Article and the Doctrine of Christ's Deity," *Journal of Theology*, Church of the Lutheran Confession, vol. 13, no. 34, vol. 14, nos. 1-4, Sept. 1973–Dec. 1974, as cited in the CARIS *Newsletter* (PO Box 1783, Santa Ana, CA), May 1978, vol. 2, no. 2 (condensed version by Michael Van Buskirk endorsed as accurate by Kuehne in "Letters," CARIS *Newsletter*, vol. 2, no. 3).

14. Metzger, p. 79.

15. H.E. Dana and Julius R. Mantey, *A Manual Grammar of the Greek New Testament* (Toronto: Macmillan, 1957), p. 147; A.T. Robertson, *Word Pictures in the New Testament* (Nashville, TN: Broadman, 1933), vol. 6, p. 147.

16. *Kingdom Interlinear Translation*, p. 896.

17. *Make Sure of All Things, Hold Fast to What Is Fine* (WBTS, 1965), p. 364.

18. See, for example, Alston Hurd Chase and Henry Phillips Jr., *A New Introduction to Greek*, 3rd ed. (Cambridge, MA: Harvard University Press, 1972), p. 41.

19. The Society has given four *different* grammatical constructions for *ego eimi*. See Michael Van Buskirk, *The Scholastic Dishonesty of the Watchtower* (Santa Ana, CA: CARIS, 1976), p. 20.

20. *Kingdom Interlinear Translation*, p. 467.

21. James Hope Moulton and William Milligan, *The Vocabulary of the Greek New Testament* (Grand Rapids, MI: Eerdmans, 1980), p. 352; Thayer's *Greek-English Lexicon of the New Testament* (Grand Rapids, MI: Baker, 1983), p. 353; Walter Bauer's *Greek-English Lexicon of the New Testament and Other Early Christian Literature*, 2nd ed., tr. William F. Arndt and F. Wilbur Gingrich, ed. F.W. Gingrich and Frederick W. Danker (Chicago: University of Chicago Press, 1979), p. 441; and Gerhard Kittel's *Theological Dictionary of the New Testament*, tr. Geoffrey W. Bromiley (Grand Rapids, MI: Eerdmans, 1978), vol. 3, p. 816.

22. Moulton and Milligan, p. 352, citing from B.P. Grenfell and A.S. Hunt, eds., *The Oxyrhynchus Papyri* (London: 1898–1927), vol. 5, p. 840.

23. Mantey, p. 142.

24. *Kingdom Interlinear Translation*, p. 988.

25. Mantey, p. 143.

26. *Watchtower*, Mar. 1, 1975, p. 151; *Aid to Bible Understanding* (WBTS, 1971), pp. 1344, 1346.

27. *Aid to Bible Understanding*, p. 1347; *Watchtower*, Jul. 1, 1943, p. 203; Mar. 15, 1971, p. 189; Apr. 1, 1972, p. 197; Jan. 15, 1959, pp. 40-41; *The Nations Shall Know That I Am Jehovah—How?* (Brooklyn, NY: WBTS, 1971), pp. 58, 70-71.

28. *Aid to Bible Understanding*, p. 1348.

29. *Watchtower*, Sept. 1, 1979, p. 29, emphasis added.

30. Reprints of early editions of *Watchtower* are available in *Reprints of the Original Watchtower and Herald of Christ's Presence*, 1879–1916 (12 vols.), from Chicago Bible Students, Box 6016, Chicago, IL 60680.

31. Bill Cetnar, in "Former Jehovah's Witnesses Testify," *The John Ankerberg Show*, 1982.

32. "Armageddon: A Happy Beginning," www.watchtower.org/e/20051201/article_02.htm.

33. Sources of prophecies on pages 57–60 are referenced by date:
    - *1877:* N.H. Barbour and C.T. Russell, *Three Worlds and the Harvest of This World* (Rochester: Barbour and Russell, 1877), p. 17; cited in Edmond Gruss, *Jehovah's Witnesses and Prophetic Speculation* (Nutley, NJ: Presbyterian & Reformed, 1972), p. 82.
    - *1886:* *Zion's Watchtower and Herald of Christ's Presence*, Jan. 1886, p. 1 (*Reprints*, vol. 2, p. 817).
    - *1889:* C.T. Russell, *The Time Is at Hand* (Allegheny, PA: WBTS, 1889), p. 101; cited in Gruss, *Jehovah's Witnesses and Prophetic Speculation*, p. 83.
    - *1894:* *Reprints*, p. 1677.
    - *1904:* C.T. Russell, *The New Creation* (WBTS, 1904), p. 579; cited in Gruss, *Jehovah's Witnesses and Prophetic Speculation*, p. 84.
    - *1914, May:* *Watchtower*, May 1, 1914, p. 134 (*Reprints*, p. 5450).
    - *1914:* *Watchtower*, May 1, 1914, pp. 23-26.
    - *1917:* *Pastor Russell's Sermons* (WBTS, 1917), p. 676.

- *1922:* J.F. Rutherford, *Millions Now Living Will Never Die* (WBTS, 1920), pp. 97, 105, 140, in Gruss, *Jehovah's Witnesses and Prophetic Speculation,* p. 87; *Watchtower,* Sept. 1, 1922, p. 262.
- *1923: Watchtower,* Apr. 1, 1923, p. 106.
- *1930:* J.F. Rutherford, *Light* (WBTS, 1930), vol. 2, p. 327; cited in Gruss, *Jehovah's Witnesses and Prophetic Speculation,* p. 89.
- *1931:* J.F. Rutherford, *Vindication,* vol. 1 (WBTS, 1931), p. 147.
- *1933:* J.F. Rutherford, *Preparation* (WBTS, 1933), p. 11.
- *1933:* J.F. Rutherford, *Preparation,* pp. 16-18.
- *1939:* J.F. Rutherford, *Salvation* (WBTS, 1939), p. 310; cited in Gruss, *Jehovah's Witnesses and Prophetic Speculation,* p. 89.
- *1940–1943:* Copies on file. Thanks to Professor Edmond C. Gruss for supplying them.
- *1940: Messenger,* Sept. 1940, p. 6
- *1941: Watchtower,* Sept. 15, 1941, pp. 276, 288.
- *1942, Jan.: Watchtower,* Jan. 15, 1942, p. 28.
- *1942, May: Watchtower,* May 1, 1942, p. 139.
- *1943: Watchtower,* May 1, 1943, p. 139.
- *1944: Watchtower,* Sept. 1, 1944, p. 264.
- *1946: Let God Be True* (WBTS, 1946), p. 194.
- *1950: This Means Everlasting Life* (WBTS, 1950), p. 311; cited in Gruss, *Jehovah's Witnesses and Prophetic Speculation,* p. 93.
- *1953: You May Survive Armageddon into God's New World* (WBTS, 1955), p. 11, compare p. 362. This statement is from a speech given in 1953.
- *1955: You May Survive Armageddon,* p. 331.
- *1958: From Paradise Lost to Paradise Regained* (WBTS, 1958), p. 205.

34. *Awake!,* October 8, 1968, p. 23.

35. See the discussion with photo documentation in Magnani and Barret, *Dialogue with Jehovah's Witnesses,* vol. 2, pp. 53-55, and Gruss, *Jehovah's Witnesses and Prophetic Speculation,* pp. 13-15; *Then Is Finished the Mystery of God* (WBTS, 1969), pp. 364-71.

36. Sources of prophecies are referenced by date:

- *1973: True Peace and Security—From What Source?* (WBTS, 1973), p. 83.
- *1973: God's Kingdom of a Thousand Years Has Approached* (WBTS, 1973), p. 44.
- *1974, May: Kingdom Ministry* magazine, May 1974, p. 3.
- *1975: Man's Salvation Out of World Distress at Hand* (WBTS, 1975), p. 312.
- *1975: Man's Salvation,* p. 349.

37. Sources of prophecies are referenced by date:

- *1992:* "Will This World Survive?" watchtower.org/e/t19/article_01.htm;
- *2005:* "Are We Really Living in 'The Last Days'?" watchtower.org/e/20060915/article_02.htm;

- *2006:* "How Do We Know We Are in the Last Days?—Part 9" watchtower. org/e/dg/article_09.htm, accessed April 12, 2008.

38. *Man's Salvation* pp. 283-84;

39. *Man's Salvation* p. 309.

40. *Man's Salvation*, p. 287. Under oath, Hayden C. Covington, legal counsel for the Society, also admitted the prophecy was false, and that it nevertheless had to be accepted by Witnesses to preserve "unity at all costs." See transcript in Gruss, *The Jehovah's Witnesses and Prophetic Speculation*, pp. 99-101.

41. *1975 Yearbook of Jehovah's Witnesses* (WBTS, 1974), p. 76; *1975 Yearbook,* pp. 145-46; *1980 Yearbook of Jehovah's Witnesses* (WBTS, 1979), pp. 30-31.

42. *1975 Yearbook,* p. 245.

43. Additional documentation of false prophecies and the Watchtower Society's suppression of vital information can be found in Gruss, *The Jehovah's Witnesses and Prophetic Speculation*, and in former 25-year member Carl Olof Jonsson's *The Gentile Times Reconsidered* (La Jolla, CA: Good News Defenders, 1983).

44. J.F. Rutherford, *The Golden Age* magazine, Jan. 18, 1933, p. 252.

45. *Aid to Bible Understanding*, p. 1060.

46. Gruss, *Apostles of Denial*, pp. 232-34, citing original documentation.

47. William and Joan Cetnar, p. 30. All but the first illustration are taken from Gruss, *We Left Jehovah's Witnesses—A Non-Prophet Organization* (Nutley, NJ: Presbyterian & Reformed, 1974), pp. 156-59, citing original documentation.

48. Gruss, *Apostles of Denial,* p. 104, compare pp. 56-66, 76; William J. Schnell, *Jehovah's Witnesses Errors Exposed* (Grand Rapids, MI: Baker, 1975), p. 13.

49. Compare the Russell-White debate of 1908; J.F. Rutherford, *Reconciliation* (WBTS, 1928), pp. 175-76; *The New World* (WBTS, 1942), pp. 360-61; *Let God Be True* (WBTS, 1946), p. 79; *The New World* (WBTS, 1952), p. 98.

50. Their official history has also been altered; see Gruss, *Apostles of Denial*, pp. 19-37.

51. *1975 Yearbook,* p. 245; J.F. Rutherford, *Prophecy* (WBTS, 1929), pp. 67-68; *Awake!*, Mar. 22, 1963.

52. Roy Goodrich, head of the Jehovah's Witness splinter sect Back to the Bible Way, discusses the Society's involvement with psychometry and radionics in his "Demonism and the Watchtower." These are spiritistic forms of medical diagnosis. See John Weldon and Zola Levitt, *Psychic Healing* (Chicago; Moody Press, 1982), pp. 53-65. The last known address of Back to the Bible Way was 517 NE Second St., Ft. Lauderdale, FL 33301.

53. For primary documentation consult Walter Martin, *Jehovah of the Watchtower* (Chicago: Moody Press, rev. ed., 1974), pp. 19-23; Gruss, *Apostles of Denial*, pp. 27, 45, 294-95; Gruss, *Jehovah's Witnesses and Prophetic Speculation*, chapter 6; Anthony Hoekema, *The Four Major Cults* (Grand Rapids, MI: Eerdmans, 1970), p. 243; Michael Van Buskirk, *The Scholastic Dishonesty of the Watchtower* p. 259; Gruss, *We Left Jehovah's Witnesses,* pp. 7, 65-66, 70, 74-75, 80-81, 83, 111, 118-19, 129; Havor Montague, "Watchtower Congregations: Communion or Conflict?" (Costa Mesa, CA: CARIS), p. 7; David Hesselgrave, ed., *Dynamic Religious Movements* (Grand Rapids, MI: Baker, 1978), p. 183. For problems on the high incidence of mental illness among Jehovah's Witnesses, see Dr. Jerry

Bergman, *The Mental Health of Jehovah's Witnesses* (Clayton, CA: Witness, Inc., 1987).

54. William and Joan Cetnar, p. 53 (compare pp. 48-55). The 1933 Johannes Greber translation *(The New Testament: A New Translation and Explanation)* is cited in, e.g., *Make Sure of All Things*, p. 489. Greber was a spirit medium who claimed his translation originated in the spirit world. His "Bible" translates John 1:1, Hebrews 1:8, and other passages the way the *NWT* does.

55. J.F. Rutherford, *Riches* (WBTS, 1936), p. 316, and *Vindication* vol. 3 (WBTS, 1932), p. 250; William and Joan Cetnar, p. 55.

56. Rutherford, *Preparation*, pp. 35-38, 67; *Watchtower*, Apr. 1, 1972, p. 200, compare Sept. 1, 1932, p. 263.

57. All from *Watchtower*, respectively Dec. 1, 1981, p. 27, and Jul. 15, 1960, p. 439; Apr. 1, 1972, p. 200; Nov. 15, 1933, p. 344; Nov. 1, 1935, p. 331; and Dec. 15, 1987, p. 7.

58. *Watchtower*, Sept. 1, 1930, p. 263, and Feb. 1, 1935, p. 41; Rutherford, *Riches*, p. 316.

59. *Jehovah's Witnesses: Proclaimers of God's Kingdom*, 1993, p. 708, from Tower Watch.org.

60. "Angels: How They Affect Us," watchtower.org/e/20060105/article_02.htm.

61. *Watchtower*, Mar. 1, 1972, p. 155, and Aug. 1, 1987, p. 19. Much of this information was supplied by Duane Magnani of Witness, Inc., PO Box 597, Clayton, CA 94517. For further information and documentation as to the Society's claim to direction and guidance from the spirit world, see Witness, Inc.'s tape "Angels of the New Light" and the text *The Heavenly Weatherman*, p. 3. A free catalogue of materials may be requested.

Section Five: Conclusion

1. Raymond Franz, *Crisis of Conscience* (Atlanta, GA: Commentary Press, 2002), p. 31. 62.

2. *Is This Life All There Is?* (WBTS, 1974), p. 99.

3. Dr. Mantey's "Distortions of the New Testament" is available as Tape T2 from Witness, Inc., PO Box 597, Clayton, CA 94517. The text of Dr. Mantey's 1974 letter is taken from Michael Van Buskirk, *The Scholastic Dishonesty of the Watchtower*, pp. 11-12. For more information on Dr. Julius Mantey, see p. 43 in this book.

ABOUT THE ANKERBERG
THEOLOGICAL RESEARCH INSTITUTE

Asking tough questions...Offering real answers

Mission Statement

The Ankerberg Theological Research Institute (ATRI) is a Christian media organization designed to investigate and answer today's critical questions concerning issues of spirituality, popular culture, and comparative religions.

> *"But in your hearts set apart Christ as Lord. Always be prepared to give an answer to everyone who asks you to give the reason for the hope that you have. But do this with gentleness and respect, keeping a clear conscience, so that those who speak maliciously against your good behavior in Christ may be ashamed of their slander."*
>
> —1 PETER 3:15-16

ATRI utilizes five strategies to accomplish this mission:

- *The John Ankerberg Show.* Our weekly half-hour TV program reaches over 147 million people in the U.S., in addition to millions more worldwide via satellite. The award-winning *John Ankerberg Show* is considered the longest-running and most-established television program available today providing answers to issues of importance to Christians (also called apologetics). Its documentary specials have been featured as nationwide television specials.

- *ATRI Radio.* ATRI reaches thousands of people through its one-hour weekend program and new one-minute daily radio commentary that is being offered on over 130 stations nationwide.

- *JohnAnkerberg.org*. ATRI's Web site reaches nearly 3 million unique visitors per year from 184 countries, providing a truly global impact. ATRI continues to utilize today's newest media formats as well, including online audio and video downloads, podcasts, blogs, and mobile technologies.

- *ATRI Resources*. In addition to over 84 combined published books and 2.5 million books sold by ATRI authors in several languages, its resources include over 2,500 online articles that have been utilized as research by some of today's best known media and academic organizations, both Christian and mainstream. In addition, ATRI offers transcripts of its TV interviews, which include thousands of hours of material from the past 28 years with top religious scholars.

- *ATRI Events*. Past speaking engagements have included Promise Keeper events, Focus on the Family seminars, and the National Apologetics Conference. Founder Dr. John Ankerberg has personally spoken to over one million people during his speaking and seminars in dozens of countries spanning five continents.

Due to ATRI's advanced research and long-standing work, founder and president Dr. John Ankerberg is regularly quoted in both Christian and mainstream media, including NBC, ABC, Daystar, and INSP, and has even testified before the U.S. Congressional Subcommittee on Financial Accountability for Christian Non-profit Organizations. A board member for many Christian media organizations, Dr. Ankerberg also serves on the board of directors for the National Religious Broadcasters Association (NRB).

THE FACTS ON SERIES
John Ankerberg and John Weldon,
with Dillon Burroughs

*To read a sample chapter of these or other Harvest House books,
go to www.harvesthousepublishers.com*